Practical Handbooks in Archaeo

HISTORIC LANDSCAPE ANALYSIS: DECIPHERING THE COUNTRYSIDE

Stephen Rippon

with a contribution by Jo Clark

2004 (Reprinted 2008)
Council for British Archaeology

First published in 2004 for the Council for British Archaeology
St Mary's House, 66 Bootham, York YO30 7BZ
1st edition reprinted 2008

British Library Cataloguing in Publication Data

A catalogue card for this book is available from the British Library

ISBN 978-1-902771-44-1

Typeset by M C Bishop at The Armatura Press
Printed by Pennine Printing Services, Ripponden, West Yorkshire
(Part of The Jarvis Print Group, Manchester)

Front cover: The canalised River Brue in the Somerset Levels, snaking past River House Farm (foreground) and looking east towards Meare (see Part Three).

Back cover: The Somerset Levels, looking east from Brent Knoll. The surface of the fields in the middle foreground are cut with spade-dug 'gripes' to aid drainage, and as such these earthworks are part of the still functioning 'historic landscape'.

Contents

List of figures

List of colour plates

List of tables

Terms and abbreviations

CCW: Countryside Council for Wales
EH: English Heritage
EN: English Nature
ERO: Essex Records Office
GIS: Geographical Information System
HLA: Historic Landuse Assessment
HLC: Historic Landscape Characterisation
HRO: Huntingdon Records Office
HS: Historic Scotland
ICOMOS: International Council on Monuments and Sites
NGR: National Grid Reference
OS: Ordnance Survey
RCAHMS: The Royal Commission on the Ancient and Historical
            Monuments of Scotland
SMR: Sites and Monuments Record
VCH: Victoria County History

Preface

The historic landscape is a remarkable record of past human achievement – the settlement patterns, field systems, woodland, industry, and communication systems that together make up our present countryside. Whilst selected features of the historic landscape have been studied by researchers for at least 50 years, only in the 1990s did the subject's whole potential start to be realised. Around the same time heritage agencies perceived the crucial importance of emphasising to planners and countryside managers the time-depth present in our countryside and the need to take this into account when making decisions and directing future policy. The use of the concept of 'Historic Landscape Characterisation' is increasingly well known, but when I was approached by the CBA to write this handbook, I was determined to move beyond this work in the planning system. I aimed for a broader consideration of how the physical fabric of the historic landscape can help local communities, students, and academics to understand the origins and development of their countryside: what I have termed here historic landscape analysis.

I would like to thank all those who have discussed their work and made the results available, notably Oscar Aldred and Chris Webster (Somerset County Council), Jo Clark and John Darlington (Lancashire County Council), Piers Dixon and Lesley Macinnes (Historic Scotland), Graham Fairclough (English Heritage), Chris Gerrard (University of Durham), Peter Herring (Cornwall County Council), David Hopkins (Hampshire County Council), Roger Kain and Richard Oliver (University of Exeter), Richard Kelly (Countryside Council for Wales), George Lambrick (Council for British Archaeology), Bob Silvester (Clywd-Powys Archaeological Trust), and Sam Turner (Devon County Council). I am especially grateful to Jo Clark for her contribution of a case study within this handbook. I would also like to thank Mike Rouillard for making sense of some of the drawings and I thank Jo Clark, Peter Herring, George Lambrick, and Sam Turner for commenting on an earlier draft of this handbook, though all views expressed here are the responsibility of the author.

Finally I must thank Rick Turner (Cadw) and the Countryside Council for Wales for establishing the Gwent Levels Historic Landscape Study: little did I know where a conversation inside a reconstructed Iron Age roundhouse on a cold, wet autumn morning would lead me!

Figure 1: The planned village of Whitson, on the reclaimed Caldicot Level in south-east Wales. This landscape is a typical palimpsest. The Caldicot Level was transformed by reclamation from intertidal saltmarshes to fertile agricultural land and, along with the creation of the planned single-row village on the edge of a funnel-shaped common (centre left), this was probably part of the 'Marcher' lords' policy of increasing productivity on the estates they acquired following the Norman Conquest of south Wales. Following the Enclosure of the Common by Act of Parliament a new road was laid out to the west (left) of the old common edge, with the result that the village is set back from the road. Sprawling industrial expansion threatens this remarkable landscape, but its national importance is now recognised in the Register of Landscapes of Outstanding Importance in Wales *(photo: the author)*

Figure 2: Places referred to in the text. Note that distinctive pays, *such as the Cotswolds, Exmoor, and the Weald are often divided between several counties (drawing: the author)*

PART ONE
UNDERSTANDING REGIONAL VARIATION IN
LANDSCAPE CHARACTER

England is an old country: ..more deeply conditioned by its past than perhaps
any of us realise ..England is also a varied country, one of the most varied in
the world in relation to its size: and this fact, too has everywhere left its imprint
on our past ..Antiquity and diversity: these, then, are two of the hallmarks of
the English landscape and English society (Everitt 1985, 1–2).

INTRODUCTION

Our rich and varied countryside

The character of our countryside – the locally distinctive patterns of fields, roads,
settlements, woodland, moorland, industry etc – is one of the richest parts of our
heritage. As early as the 1950s scholars such as Hoskins (1955,14) recognised that it
provides a remarkable record of past human achievement – the 'richest historical
record we possess' – though it was only from the 1990s that the term 'historic
landscape' was widely used to reflect the time-depth present within our modern
countryside. Another key feature is its diversity and complexity, as reflected by
Everitt's (1985, 2) comparison of the landscape in Kent, Leicestershire, and
Westmorland:

> The map of Leicestershire appears like a series of spiders' webs: the roads
> radiate neatly from the villages in a relatively open network, often more or less
> straight for considerable stretches, eventually converging on the nine or ten
> main roads of the county, which themselves converge in regular lines on
> Leicester itself – the fattest spider in the centre of the largest web. The fields
> are often large and straight-sided; the villages are large and nucleated. Despite
> seventeenth- and eighteenth-century enclosures, many farmhouses still stand
> in village streets, and it is rare to find any in the fields which date from much
> before the eighteenth century. In the rural areas of Kent – let alone
> Westmorland – there is no such regularity. The road-map is more like a maze, a
> tangle of endlessly twisting lanes sunk between wooded banks often too narrow
> for two vehicles to pass. ..There is no obvious urban centre, like Leicester, but
> a series of smaller towns, like Canterbury, Maidstone, and Ashford. The fields
> are small and irregular, broken up with woods and copses, and peppered with
> isolated farms.

This handbook is concerned with how we can systematically describe such local and
regional variations in landscape character, and understand when and how these
patterns emerged (eg Figs 1 and 3).

Figure 3: The Somerset Levels: strongly contrasting historic landscapes in close proximity. Top: Pool Farm and Ham Farm, Kingston Seymour, Somerset, looking south-west towards the Bristol Channel. The dispersed settlement pattern and irregular field systems result from gradual, piecemeal colonisation of this area of former intertidal saltmarsh, starting by the 10th century and continuing throughout the medieval period (for location see Fig 27.2; photo: the author). Bottom: Mark Moor, Somerset: a carefully planned Parliamentary Enclosure (1784) landscape of former common 'waste', looking south-east towards Glastonbury and Street (for location see Fig 27.2; photo: the author)

Past- and future-oriented analysis of the historic landscape and 'Historic Landscape Characterisation'

Throughout the 20th century archaeologists, historians, and historical geographers have been studying the origins and development of the British countryside, with approaches varying from the detailed examination of a specific location (often a parish or estate), to broad national or county-based studies of specific individual facets of the landscape (notably settlement patterns, field systems, and farming regimes). Although some use was made of evidence contained within the present countryside, this was usually in a highly selective way. The physical fabric of what we now call the 'historic landscape' – the countryside either as it survives today, or as it was first mapped in a comprehensive fashion in the 19th century – was rarely itself the focus for the systematic study of human interaction with the environment over large areas.

The term 'historic landscape analysis' is used here to embrace a series of approaches that all focus on how the present countryside came into being. It is also a means of integrating a wide range of source material in order to understand the processes of landscape change. The multidisciplinary study of particular areas of countryside is not new, but there are five things that distinguish the approach advocated here from many older studies: the historic landscape as a source itself and as a means of integrating other evidence, inclusivity, focus, scale, and understanding process from form.

1. **The historic landscape as a source itself and as a means of integrating other evidence:** the core source of information in historic landscape analysis is the physical fabric of the historic landscape itself. This provides the ideal spatial and temporal framework for the careful integration of a wide range of other evidence, notably archaeological material, documentary and cartographic sources, and place- and field-names. Vernacular architecture also has enormous potential though this is yet to be realised (though see the Shapwick Project: Aston and Gerrard 1999; SVBRG 1996). *Inter*disciplinarity is where these different strands of evidence are worked on simultaneously, and seamlessly woven together to give one landscape history (in contrast to so many *multi*disciplinary studies where the archaeological, historical etc evidence are discussed in separate chapters).

2. **Inclusivity:** historic landscape analysis is applied evenly and systematically to every part of a pre-determined study area of whatever size (parish, county, Ordnance Survey grid square etc). The approach embraces modern as well as ancient, semi-natural as well as man-made, typical as well as unusual/unique.

3. **Period and focus:** while embracing all facets of a predetermined block of countryside, the focus of this approach is on the origins and development of the modern countryside. It starts with the present and works back (a 'retrogressive' approach) until the period when the fundamental features of the historic landscape came into being is reached. While this means that the focus of study in most areas will be the medieval and post-medieval periods, in a few important areas the dominant framework of today's countryside is earlier. This is not the same as 'total landscape archaeology/history' where all the archaeology/history of

the study area is described 'because it is there', even though it makes no contribution to the character of the *present* countryside.

4. **Scale:** although mapping historic landscape character can be useful for an individual parish, its full potential for understanding why the character of the countryside varies over time and space can also be realised when applied uniformly and systematically at a regional, county or even potentially national scale.

5. **Understanding process from form:** because of the large areas that are subject to analysis, every individual settlement, field system etc cannot be studied in depth. The landscape has to be broken down into a series of *generic* types based on their morphology/character, for which research elsewhere may by analogy suggest its origins and development.

The research outlined above can be regarded as 'past-oriented' (Bloemers 2002); the focus is on understanding the processes of landscape change, and how the present countryside came into being. The 1990s also saw the initiation of a series of closely related 'future-oriented' projects that, while still falling under the 'umbrella' of historic landscape analysis, have a particular focus on planning and management in the countryside. This work recognises that everywhere has historic character even if it is recent (and including most 'semi-natural' environments), and that such character is all around us and plays a vital part in shaping our wider cultural environment. This view also recognises that our surroundings are continually changing both physically and in terms of our perception. The terms 'past-oriented' and 'future-oriented' are preferred here to saying 'research-related' and 'planning related', because work carried out in a planning or management context is itself important research. A series of different initiatives to assess historic landscape character are underway in England, Scotland, and Wales (described in more detail in Part Two). English Heritage is working with local authorities to produce a series of county-wide 'Historic Landscape Characterisation Projects' (HLCs), while Historic Scotland/The Royal Commission on the Ancient and Historical Monuments of Scotland are carrying out a similar exercise called 'Historic Landuse Assessment' north of the border. It is important to stress that 'Historic Landscape Characterisation' as it is being practised in the English Heritage sponsored projects is not the same as the more holistic concept of historic landscape analysis that is the subject of this handbook.

In terms of heritage management and conservation this work in England and Scotland represents a move to go further than designating selected 'sites', and to recognise that people value the historic character of places in much more general terms. In Wales, however, a different approach has been developed with Cadw and the Countryside Council for Wales having identified specific areas as being of particular importance and including them in *The Register of Landscapes of Historic Interest in Wales*. These individual landscapes are now the subject of another form of characterisation (also described in Part Two). These projects are all primarily concerned with informing planners and countryside managers of what, in cultural/historic terms, are the key character defining features of particular landscapes across whole regions/counties. While seeking to provide an understanding of how present landscape character came into being, such exercises are primarily 'future-oriented' (Bloemers

4

2002), though a database carefully constructed for this purpose still has great value for 'past-oriented' research (eg Somerset: see Part Three).

The scope of this handbook

The English Heritage, Historic Scotland/RCAHMS and Cadw/CCW Projects introduced above all have their own methodologies and this handbook is not intended as an alternative; rather it is aimed at a wider audience and is designed to show how the broad principles of historic landscape analysis can be used alongside landscape archaeology and history. Once we learn how to 'read the landscape', anyone from professional academics to local archaeological/historical societies can start to unravel the history of the countryside and appreciate the many factors that have influenced its present day character. This handbook is intended as a guide to some of the many ways that the historic character and development of the countryside can be analysed, though it is important to stress that it is *not* a manual describing a single methodology; there is not, nor should be, just one 'technique' of historic landscape analysis, for just as the historic landscape itself is so rich and varied, so are the reasons for studying it, and the approaches that can be used.

Following this Introduction, the rest of Part One begins by outlining some of the major regional variations within the British countryside, and shows how historic landscape analysis has emerged from a long tradition of research across a number of disciplines. What contributes to historic character is then introduced in terms of a series of physical and conceptual components/themes that together combine to give a range of generic historic landscape types, and which in turn combine in different ways to produce unique character areas. Other facets of the countryside, such as its place- and field-names, use of building materials and its relationship to abandoned 'relict' remains of earlier landscapes, are then introduced, followed by a consideration of the concept of 'natural beauty' and the contribution of people to landscape character. Finally, a case study of the parish of Hadleigh, in Essex, is used to illustrate these basic principles, and to show how the character of the historic landscape is the product of interaction between the natural environment and human communities giving rise to a series of different processes and trajectories of change.

Part Two of this handbook considers the main approaches towards historic landscape analysis currently in use, both as a means to enlighten planners/countryside managers and as a research tool. The contrasting 'future-oriented' approaches towards historic landscape characterisation of heritage organisations in England, Scotland and Wales are illustrated, before an examination of some of the broader ways through which analysis of the historic landscape can be used as part of 'past-oriented' research into landscape history.

Part Three examines some of the applications and uses of historic landscape analysis. Examples of English Heritage sponsored HLCs in Cornwall and Lancashire are used to show some of the different methodologies, and what these projects have told us about the evolution of those landscapes, while the Somerset HLC is used as a springboard for a more in-depth case study of just one of potentially many research themes that can arise from HLC. The fourth case study presents an example of a detailed parish-based study of the medieval manor of Meare in the Somerset Levels, illustrating the integration of documentary material with the historic landscape in order to reconstruct the progress of landscape change over time.

Finally, in Part Four certain key points of good practice are identified.

Key features of this handbook are the case studies and illustrations. Whilst clearly relating to specific locations, they are intended to make *general* points regarding sources, methodologies, and interpretations. Several of the examples reflect the work of teams in Cornwall, Hampshire, and Lancashire County Councils, Historic Scotland/ The Royal Commission on the Ancient and Historical Monuments of Scotland, and the Clwyd-Powys Archaeological Trust (Wales), which are all models of good practice and easily available through a variety of publication media. The remaining case studies are the work of the author. While the majority present new explorations of the origins and development of particular landscapes, several also develop new interpretations of earlier work, reminding us that analysis of the historic landscape is a means of stimulating further research, not simply an end in itself. No historic landscape analysis should be left on a shelf to gather dust as interpretations are liable to be updated in the light of further research.

A note on townscapes

As it is currently practised, historic landscape analysis has been mostly applied to rural areas and these will be the focus of this handbook. The historic character of our urban areas is, however, just as varied and complex as the countryside and similarly reflects the different trajectories and agencies of change (see Fig 4). As with the rural countryside, historical geographers have a long history of exploring the evolution of 'urban landscapes' through the careful analysis of plan and street layouts and standing buildings (eg Lilley 2002, 138–77), and there is ample scope for integrating archaeological evidence with the often abundant historical and cartographic sources (eg Leech 1975; 1981; Aston and Leech 1977; Phillpotts 1999). The principles of historic landscape analysis are also now being applied to the townscapes in a number of areas, including Cornwall, Lancashire and Merseyside, in order to establish the historic character of what survives today. Any future edition of this handbook would hope to report on this work.

REGIONAL VARIATION IN LANDSCAPE CHARACTER AND THE TRAJECTORIES OF CHANGE

What is often so highly valued about our landscape – what gives communities their sense of place and identity – is local character and distinctiveness, and before describing how we can unravel the story behind these regional differences, it might be useful to outline some of the most fundamental divisions in landscape character within the British countryside. In terms of the physical environment, the British landscape contains marked variations in topography, climate and soils. Travelling around our island, one also cannot avoid being struck by the diversity in its cultural landscape. Archaeological and palaeoenvironmental work has shown that across Britain the landscape was largely cleared of woodland and extensively settled by the end of the Roman period. In places, indeed, today's countryside is a direct descendent of that

6

Figure 4: Exeter, Devon: contrasting urban townscapes with distinctive characters to which HLC could be applied (see Henderson 1999 and Oliver 1999 for an introduction to the history and development of Exeter). Top: Southernhay: a late 18th-century 'middle-class' development immediately outside the city walls, with two rows of elegant town houses either side of an open space. These buildings no longer serve their original function as domestic residences, now being used as offices (photo: the author). Bottom: Newtown: mid-19th-century working-class suburb. The buildings retain their original domestic function (photo: the author)

prehistoric and Romano-British settlement (eg West Penwith in Cornwall, the East Anglian boulder clays, and the south corner of Essex: Herring 1993; Williamson 1987, Rippon 1991). In most places, however, the essential character of today's countryside is more recent. An obvious contrast is between a zone running from eastern and central/ lowland Scotland, through north-east England, the Midlands and down to the south coast, which along with parts of southern Wales has a settlement pattern broadly characterised by nucleated villages (Fig 5). This central zone can be contrasted with south-east England, the south-west Peninsula, the west and north-west of England, most of Wales and the Highlands of Scotland, which have a landscape characterised by more sprawling patterns of settlement. This is a very broad generalisation, but if one goes back in time, these differences were even greater, and the cultural processes that led to their creation become clearer. From the 16th century, topographical writers such as Leland were well aware of the distinction between the 'champion' landscape of open fields and nucleated villages in Midland England, and the 'bosky' or 'woodland' landscape of hedged fields and scattered settlement to the south-east and west. In 1685, for example, the writer Aubrey (1685, 104–7) drew a clear distinction between the 'vast champion fields' of Malmesbury and Chippenham in the 'northern vales' of Wiltshire, and the sheep pastures of the 'southern Downes' (Salisbury Plain), while in 1795 Billingsley (1798) contrasted the 'meadow, pasture and arable intermix in high cultivation' of south-east Somerset (its 'champion lands'), with the 'rich grazing and dairy lands' in the west and north of the county. Historic landscape analysis is not just a means of *describing* such local and regional variation in the character of the countryside, but also helps us to *understand* how it came into being.

Rackham (1986), in his seminal work *The History of the Countryside*, has produced one of the most accessible examples of how these fundamental historical differences in the British landscape have shaped the countryside of today (Fig 6; Table 1). He divided lowland England between two zones of 'ancient countryside' (in the South East and West), which equate with the 'woodland' landscapes noted by early topographical writers, and 'planned countryside' (in the Midland zone) resulting from the enclosure of open fields in the 'champion' region. This simple division of the English landscape has long been recognised (eg Gonner 1912), and most recently has been mapped by Roberts and Wrathmell (2000a; 2002) as their 'South-Eastern', 'Northern and Western' and 'Central' Provinces respectively (Fig 5). These different landscapes were the product of different trajectories and timescales of change and episodes of cataclysm, continuity and colonisation (Roberts and Wrathmell 2002, 12–14). Rackham's scheme provides an excellent starting point from which to understand the link between historical process and present landscape character as he is careful to distinguish between *modern characteristics* of the two areas and *historic differences*: the two are not necessarily the same (Table 1).

The origins of landscapes characterised by nucleated villages and open fields have been much debated, and it is now clear that they replaced landscapes associated with more dispersed settlement patterns (Foard 1978; Hall 1981; Rowley 1981; Lewis *et al* 1997; Brown and Foard 1998; Roberts and Wrathmell 2002; Williamson 2003). In the Midlands and central southern England this reorganisation of the landscape, variously called the 'great replanning' and the 'village moment', appears to have occurred around the 9th/10th centuries, while in northern England and parts of southern Wales 'villagisation' may have been a post-Conquest phenomenon. There is little agreement as to why it occurred, with socio-economic explanations – such as

TABLE 1: Highly generalised key character defining features of Rackham's (1986) 'ancient' and 'planned' countryside (based on Rackham 1986 tabs 1.1 and 1.2, with additions in square brackets)

'ancient' countryside (the South East and western England)		'planned' countryside (Midland England)	
modern	*historic*	*modern*	*historic*
isolated farms, hamlets and small towns	[farmsteads, hamlets and small towns, derived from a long history of settlement growth and contraction]	villages [resulting from the 9th–12th century 'replanning'] and isolated farms [which emerged after Parliamentary Enclosure as farmers moved closer to their now consolidated landholdings]	villages [resulting from the 9th–12th century 'replanning']
[enclosed fields, mostly irregular in layout]	open fields either absent or of modest extent and enclosed before *c*.1700 [though recent research, including the HLCs in Cornwall and Devon, are challenging this: see Part 3]	[enclosed fields, mostly rectilinear/planned in layout resulting from Parliamentary Enclosure]	strong tradition of open fields lasting into the Enclosure Act period [18th–19th century]
hedges mainly mixed, not straight	most hedges ancient	hedges mainly hawthorn, and straight [having been planted following Parliamentary Enclosure, the plants coming from nurseries]	[very few hedges in a landscape of open fields]
roads many, and not straight	[roads many, and not straight]	roads few, and straight [resulting from Parliamentary Enclosure]	[different network of roads to that created during Parliamentary Enclosure]
many public footpaths	[many footpaths/rights of way]	few footpaths	[different network of footpaths/rights of way to that created during Enclosure]
many woods, often small	many woods, often small	woods absent, or few and large	woods absent, or few and large

Figure 5: The major areas of nucleated settlement in Britain (from Roberts 1987, fig 1.1), and the three 'settlement provinces' of England (from Roberts and Wrathmell 2002, fig 1.4: redrawing: the author)

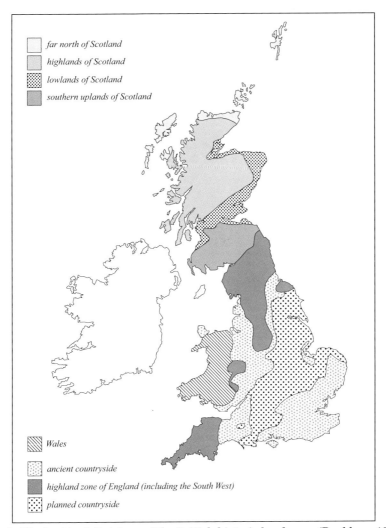

far north of Scotland

highlands of Scotland

lowlands of Scotland

southern uplands of Scotland

Wales

ancient countryside

highland zone of England (including the South West)

planned countryside

Figure 6: The basic subdivisions of the British historic landscape (Rackham 1986, fig 1.3). The 'planned' and 'ancient' countryside divisions correspond to the 'champion' and 'woodland' districts described by early topographical writers (redrawn by Mike Rouillard)

estate owners and communities restructuring their landed resources in order to increase productivity at a time of rising population, growing economic activity and increasing royal exactions – contrasting with environmentally deterministic factors such as the ability to increase arable production on certain types of soil.

Although the essential *medieval* character defining features of this 'Central Province' were created over a relatively short space of time, it is possible that these distinctive village landscapes were created in what was already an area that possessed a different character to adjacent areas. Roberts and Wrathmell (2000b, 27–38) have

11

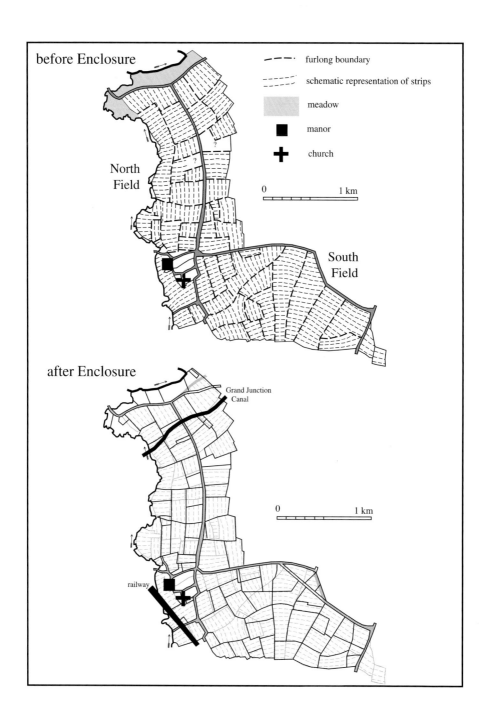

before Enclosure

- - - furlong boundary

schematic representation of strips

meadow

■ manor

✝ church

North Field

0   1 km

South Field

after Enclosure

Grand Junction Canal

railway

0   1 km

12

noted that it corresponds very closely to the area of England that the Domesday Book and pre-Conquest place-names indicate was the most extensively cleared of woodland even before it was subject to the creation of villages. The extent to which individual earlier features affected the form taken by the landscapes of villages and open fields is unclear, though if our present village locations represent an element of the dispersed settlement pattern that was otherwise swept away, then part of the Midland landscape owes its origins to the early medieval period or even earlier. In places there are similarly hints that earlier field boundaries may have been reused/incorporated into the open field systems (eg Taylor and Fowler 1978; Upex 2002; Oosthuizen 2003; Gerrard and Aston forthcoming, trench 2700/N).

The open fields, which were presumably created at the same time as the villages, were themselves swept away through a long process of enclosure, initially by agreement in the late medieval/early post-medieval periods, and later by Act of Parliament in the 18th/19th centuries (Figs 6–7; see Johnson 1996, 44–69 and Williamson 2002a for recent discussions of this phenomenon). In these Midland parishes, therefore, the landscape of today is largely the product of two episodes of replanning: 9th/10th-century 'villagisation' and later Parliamentary Enclosure, perhaps with some elements of the pre-9th-century settlement pattern preserved by the location (though not the character) of the villages. In contrast, large parts of Britain were not subject to the processes that led to creation of nucleated villages and open fields, and here the medieval landscape was broadly characterised by more dispersed settlement patterns with a mixture of enclosed and open/subdivided fields. The historic landscapes in these areas are, as a result, even more of a palimpsest. In localised parts of East Anglia and the South East, for example, later prehistoric, Romano-British and early medieval planned, coaxial field systems appear to be preserved within the present historic landscape (eg Williamson 1987; 2002b; 2003; Rippon 1991; Higham 1992, fig 5.15; Warner 1996), while in the far west of Cornwall the present pattern of fields and settlements could date back to the Iron Age (Herring 1993; 1998, 26–7). This remote corner of Cornwall escaped the restructuring of the landscape of the South West associated with the emergence of a regionally distinctive system of agriculture known as convertible husbandry which developed during the later 1st millennium AD, which suggests that the Midlands was not the only region to see landscape reorganisation at around this time (see Cornwall case study in Part Three).

In contrast to these landscapes whose essential characteristics date back at least a thousand years (or in some cases two thousand or more), in Scotland the recent Historic Landuse Assessment has shown that vast areas were extensively remodelled in the 18th/19th-century agricultural 'improvements' (see Part Two). In England and Wales many upland areas also saw major changes in the post-medieval period. Discussion of Parliamentary Enclosure so far has focused on the extinction of lowland open fields, though in upland areas landscapes were also transformed at this time as commons and

---

Figure 7: Bradwell, Buckinghamshire: a classic 'Midland-style' parish of the Central Province/Champion landscape (Croft and Mynard 1993, figs 26–7). Top: before enclosure: a single nucleated village, and an open two-field system that covered virtually the whole parish (drawing: the author). Bottom: after enclosure in 1788: a new set of enclosed fields were created that in part respected the earlier furlongs but elsewhere ignored them; note how the railway and canal are stratigraphically later than the fields (based on the Tithe Map of 1839; drawing: the author)

wastes were divided into large, neatly walled fields often with characteristic field barns. In counties such as Cumbria nearly a quarter of the county was enclosed by Act of Parliament, of which a tiny amount was arable open field, and when these upland enclosures are mapped the areas of ancient enclosure form small 'islands' of settlement within a 'sea' of what was once open land (eg Whyte 2000, fig 1; and see Lancashire case study in Part Three). This is a marked reversal of the situation in lowland areas where the commons and droveways (with their wide strips of roadside waste) that survived into the post-medieval period were just small 'islands' within a large 'sea' of agricultural land (eg see Hadleigh case study below: Fig 15). In all these cases, the regularly arranged post-medieval enclosures are often easily identifiable, and their delimitation at an early stage of a historic landscape analysis allows attention to then focus on those older landscapes of greater complexity (eg Exmoor: Fig 18).

APPROACHES TO STUDYING REGIONAL VARIATION IN LANDSCAPE CHARACTER

The various approaches to historic landscape analysis have developed from a long history of studying regional variation in the character of the British countryside. Perhaps the first systematic overview came about in *c* 1800 with the Board of Agriculture Reports on the state of farming in each English county (eg Tuke 1800), which were brought together in a series of summary volumes that identified distinct regions based on physical topography, soils, climate, and farming practice (Marshall 1808; 1818a–d). The partially surviving Tithe Files of *c* 1840 give a more detailed picture of mid-19th-century agriculture in many regions including the proportions of common land, woodland, pasture, and arable, and the crops that were grown (Kain 1986).

Despite the clear recognition of regional diversity by early topographical writers (see above) and these Board of Agriculture reports, variation in the historic character of the landscape is hardly evident in the seminal writings on medieval society by late 19th- and early 20th-century historians such as Seebohm (1883), Vinogradoff (1892; 1905; 1908) and Maitland (1911; 1921). Based on their work one could be forgiven for assuming that most of the English population lived in villages, and cultivated various types of open field, and it was only in Gray's (1915) *English Field Systems* that the extent of variation in the medieval landscape started to be appreciated. He recognised a series of regional field systems and cropping practices – the Midlands, Celtic, Kentish, East Anglian, and Lower Thames basin 'systems' – and made it clear that the regularly arranged Midland-style open field landscapes covered less than half of England and Wales. Gray attributed the origins of open fields and nucleated villages, to the early Anglo-Saxon migrations, with the remaining landscapes being seen as later creations through woodland clearance. This attributing of cultural change to immigration is seen throughout early and mid-20th-century archaeology including Fox's (1932) seminal work *The Personality of Britain*, though he also emphasised the role of a fundamental division of the physical landscape: the two-fold upland/lowland divide. Building upon Mackinder's (1907) earlier work, this simple division was identified as lying roughly along a line between the estuaries of the rivers Tees and Exe, dividing the older and harder Palaeozoic rocks to the north and west, and younger, softer rocks to the south and east.

The 1950s–60s saw two major projects on historical material that allowed the more detailed mapping of aspects of landscape character, notably population and agriculture. Firstly, Darby and his collaborators completed a series of county studies in the *Domesday Geography of England* series (Darby 1977). The regions he identified were largely determined by physical geography, but clear variations in agricultural systems were also discernable. Secondly, in preparing material for the *Agrarian History of England and Wales*, Thirsk (1967b) and Emery (1967) used probate inventories to identify a series of 'farming regions' in 16th-century England. Whilst in very broad terms a south/east–north/west division is evident between zones with predominantly mixed and pastoral farming respectively, it is the extent of very localised diversity that is most striking. These 16th-century farming regions were seen as largely resulting from changes in the agrarian economy during the late medieval period, though Campbell (2000) has since used 13th- and 14th-century records to identify significant regional variation in landuse by c 1300.

The 1950s–60s also saw the emergence of medieval archaeology as a serious discipline, with the study of deserted settlements, notably villages and moated sites, forming a major part (Beresford 1954; Beresford and Hurst 1971; Aberg 1978). Another aspect of the medieval landscape that received renewed attention from the 1950s was its field systems. Despite Gray's demonstration that not all of England and Wales had Midland-style open fields, a number of regional studies outside the Midlands (eg Yorkshire: Harris 1959; Northumberland: Butlin 1964; Kent: Baker 1965), and Baker and Butlin's (1973) major overview *Studies of Field Systems in the British Isles*, research into medieval field systems remained focused on the origins and development of landscapes characterised by subdivided/open fields (eg Thirsk 1964; Dodgshon 1980; Rowley 1981).

The 1970s marked a 'high tide' of interest in mapping spatial and temporal variations in different aspects of the British landscape: the classic age of historical geography (Darby 1973; Dodgshon and Butlin 1978). The analysis of data contained within medieval taxations, such as those of 1334, 1377, and 1524–25, for example, led to the mapping of regional variations in population densities and wealth, which in many areas fluctuated significantly over time (eg Baker 1973; Donkin 1973; Emery 1973). The distribution of towns, markets, and rural industries also showed marked regional variations that must have had a profound effect on the wider landscape character (Finch 2002). One example is the cloth industry that in the 13th century was spread across much of England, but which during the late medieval period consolidated into a restricted number of regions such as Devon, the Cotswolds, and East Anglia (Figs 8–9). This reminds us of three things: firstly, that some rural landscapes contained a significant industrial component, such as iron production in the Black Country (Everitt 1979, 13); secondly, that industry generally was a more significant contributor, albeit at a low level, to landscape character in *many* more areas than one might imagine (Devon and Kent would not be regarded by many as being industrial counties yet in the 1860s, industrial workers accounted for 27% and 22% of the population respectively: Everitt 1985, 6); and thirdly, that while many archaeologists have focused upon understanding the early origins of the medieval landscape, even outside the areas of Parliamentary Enclosure the character of today's historic landscape was often profoundly shaped by changes in the late medieval and post-medieval period. In Cornwall and Devon, for example, the highly dispersed settlement patterns that characterise large parts of the countryside have

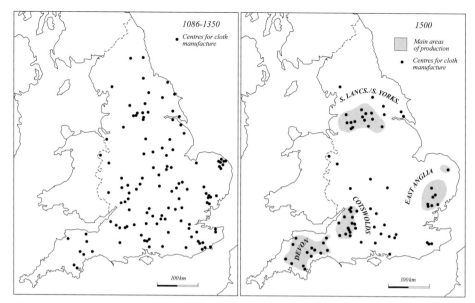

Figure 8: The character of the rural countryside was not simply shaped through agriculture. In the past, a wide range of industrial activities were located in rural areas, such as textile production. In the high Middle Ages, c 1300, woollen production occurred across much of lowland England, whereas in the late medieval period it became concentrated in a limited number of regions (Donkin 1973, fig 28 and Baker 1973, fig 49). The specialisation in landuse led to the conversion of arable to pasture, fossilising ridge and furrow in the former open fields, while the wealth it created is manifested in magnificent 'wool churches' that still dominate the landscape in some areas (redrawn by Mike Rouillard)

been shown to result from the late medieval shrinkage of what were formerly more nucleated settlements (Beresford 1964; Fox 1989), while specialist fishing villages that characterise the coastal areas are similarly only late medieval and post-medieval in origin (Fox 2001).

Though Crawford (1953, 51) said, 'the surface of England is a palimpsest, a document that has been written on and erased over and over again; it is the business of the field archaeologist to decipher it', and Hoskins (1955, 14) described the landscape as 'the richest historical record we possess', little progress was made for several decades in realising the potential of the historic landscape for research. Though some historians and historical geographers analysed modern settlement plans and field systems, and there was some integration of this morphological evidence with documentary sources (eg Sheppard 1966; Sylvester 1969), there was little sense that the fabric of the present landscape as a whole was of historic interest and value, and that it could be 'read' using archaeological techniques of spatial analysis. Archaeologists, meanwhile, had been concerned with individual 'sites', though by the 1970s the widespread adoption of aerial photography, fieldwalking and large-scale rescue excavations led to an expansion in the scale at which they worked. 'Sites' were now recognised as forming but a small part of wider buried or relict 'landscapes', and as the whole landscape became a focus for study,

Figure 9: The Stroud Valley, in the Cotswolds, Gloucestershire. One of the areas that saw a regional specialisation in textile production during the late medieval period, the historic landscape of the Stroud Valley still has a strongly industrial feel (photo: the author)

it was increasingly appreciated that there was also a vast amount of information locked up within the fabric of the present countryside. So it was that 'landscape archaeology' emerged as a discipline in the 1970s with the study of the present pattern of settlements, fields, roads etc, as an integral part (Aston and Rowley 1974; Aston 1985). It was only in the late 1980s, however, that the specific concept of 'historic landscape' emerged in both the worlds of planning and research (eg Hooke 1988; Lambrick 1992; Council for British Archaeology 1993; Rippon and Turner 1993; Cornwall County Council 1994; Fairclough 1995).

A common feature of much landscape research is its focus on particular sources of evidence, aspects of the landscape that have gone out of use (eg deserted medieval villages), or individual components of the landscape such as the patterns of roads, settlements, and field systems (eg Taylor 1975, 1979; Rowley 1981; Hindle 1982). Throughout the 20th century historians in particular also wrote about the agrarian economy and society without apparently feeling the need to reconstruct the landscapes they were discussing – the reader was provided with at best a single map showing the major places referred to in the text (eg Finberg 1951). A more holistic approach, however, has been developed by scholars such as Hoskins, Everitt, Phythian-Adams, and Fox at Leicester University's Department of English Local History. A key concept in their work is that of *pays*, a French term for areas that possess their own innate identity (Everitt 1979; 1985; 1986, 5–6, 43–68; Braudel 1988; Thirsk 2000). This concept, similar to the German idea of *Landschaft* (Leighley 1963, 315–50), saw a more holistic concept of landscape that, while still having a strong element of environmental and geographical determinism, also stressed the contribution of different social structures in shaping landscape character. Hoskins was perhaps the most influential 20th-century writer on landscape, and his seminal book *The Making of the English Landscape* (1955) remains a classic study of both broad regional variation and local distinctiveness. Though he did not map *pays*, he was keenly aware of their existence, not just in terms of distinctive physical regions (such as marshes, fens, and moors), but the cultural landscape, for example contrasting the large-scale open fields of the Midlands with the 'miniature' open field systems of Devon and Oxfordshire (Hoskins 1955, 82–3). *Pays* can be understood in various senses:

- *generic* types of *cultural* landscape (eg those characterised by slate mining, villages, and open fields, or resulting from woodland assarting)
- *generic* types of *topographically* defined areas (eg 'downlands', 'heathlands', 'lowland vales', 'fenlands', and 'moorlands')
- *specific locations* with a unique identity defined by the *cultural* landscape (eg the iron-producing Black Country in Staffordshire, coal mining districts such has Merthyr Tydfil in South Wales, and distinctive farming regions such as Felden and Arden in Warwickshire)
- *specific locations* with a unique identity defined by the *topography* (eg Breckland, the Vale of Clywd, or the Yorkshire Dales).

Some such *pays* can be very extensive, such as the *c* 6,500 sq km Boulder Clay plateau stretching from Hertfordshire to East Anglia (Warner 1996; Williamson 2003), while others are relatively small and closely defined (eg the *c* 50 sq km Caldicot Level: Fig 20).

Crucial to understanding how the countryside has developed is the pattern of social territories within which it was created and managed on a day-to-day basis. All to often archaeologists, historians, and historical geographers have used counties as the units within which to study the landscape as they are of a convenient size and have a resonance with the public (eg Williamson 2002b). This emphasis on counties is regrettable as, while many of these studies provide excellent overviews of those areas, they rarely examine whole *pays* because county boundaries often go against the grain of the natural and cultural landscape. The English shires were mostly a 9th- to early 11th-century creation which in the Midlands in particular were largely artificial administrative units with little relationship to the cultural or physical landscape; it was only around the 16th century that counties became the major expression of social identity (Everitt 1979; Blair 1994, 104).

Phythian-Adams (1993) has explored the impact that the physical landscape had on human territoriality through his concept of 'cultural provinces' based on river-drainage basins and the all-important watersheds. These watersheds represent 'identifiable lines of punctuation in the landscape.characterised for long stretches by bands of primarily pastoral countryside.which, in historic times at least, probably originates as zones for intercommoning, almost invariably.settled late from opposite directions, and then to be occupied far less densely than the more heavily populated heartlands on their either sides' (Phythian-Adams 1993, 11). The arrangement of territories that run from river to watershed, or lowland to upland, has been a recurrent one throughout human history (eg the 'concave landscape' model developed by Coles and Coles (1986, fig 34) for the way that prehistoric human communities used the wetland resources of the Somerset Levels in the context of a wider landscape exploitation strategy). During the early medieval period, the strategy of incorporating both upland and lowland within a territory was central to the principle behind the 'multiple estate' structure documented in Wales (eg Jones 1979), while discrete *regios* such as the Rodings in Essex (Bassett 1997) and Swaledale in Yorkshire (Fleming 1998) similarly used watersheds for their boundaries. These landscapes of large territories/estates frequently fragmented into smaller units, but the mapping of the medieval vills/townships that were created (usually reflected by ecclesiastical parishes) show that communities often still occupied territories that straddled different zones (see Hadleigh, case study below Fig 15; and for Greater Exmoor: Fig 18).

Such 'resource optimisation' approaches to landscape exploitation are not uncommon, and remind us that in order to properly understand the landscape, we must study it using the territories that were perceived as significant by past communities themselves. Therefore, these extensive 'cultural provinces', medium-sized *regios*, and individual townships are all in their own way ideal units within which to study the landscape as they had a practical existence in the past in terms of how resources and potential were exploited; they were the day-to-day social, economic, and agrarian units within which the countryside was managed and the historic landscape was created.

THE COMPOSITION OF A HISTORIC LANDSCAPE: ELEMENTS, COMPONENTS, TYPES, ZONES, AND AREAS

Deconstructing a historic landscape

Different landscape character results from variations in the form and spatial arrangement of a wide range of features reflecting the different means by which human communities achieved subsistence, communication, recreation, and security at various periods in the past. One way of thinking about these landscapes is as a series of individual **elements** (eg field boundaries) or **parcels** (eg a field), which combine in various ways to form certain discrete **components** or 'themes' within the landscape (the collective term for a group of elements/parcels of the same function, eg field system). The form of each component, and the way that they articulate with other components, determines historic landscape character, and a distinctive and repeated combination of components define a generic historic landscape character **type**. These types can be very localised in their extent, and they in turn combine in different ways to define the unique character **areas** that make up the British countryside (Table 2).

Historic landscape components

An experienced practitioner of historic landscape analysis can identify character types without the need to disaggregate the landscape into its separate components, though the study of these individual themes within a landscape remains a useful stepping-

19

TABLE 2: Schematic examples of historic landscape elements, parcels, components, types and areas

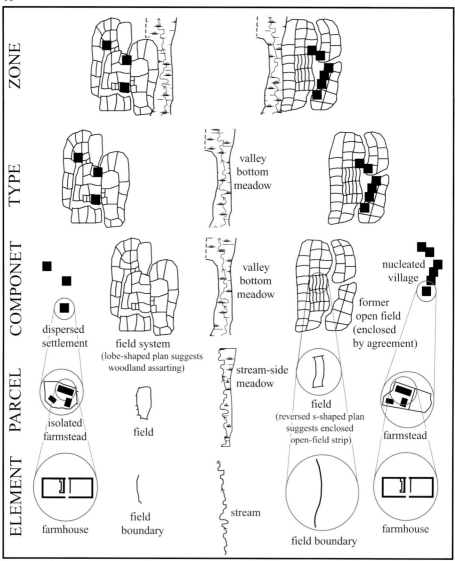

ZONE

TYPE

COMPONET

PARCEL

ELEMENT

valley
bottom
meadow

valley
bottom
meadow

stream-side
meadow

stream

dispersed
settlement

field system
(lobe-shaped plan suggests
woodland assarting)

isolated
farmstead

field

field
boundary

farmhouse

nucleated
village

former
open field
(enclosed
by agreement)

field
(reversed s-shaped plan
suggests enclosed
open-field strip)

farmstead

field boundary

farmhouse

stone towards a more holistic understanding of its origins and development. In particular, this approach provides a link with more traditional landscape archaeology and
history approaches that have often focused on individual themes such as settlement or
field systems, and allows the key 'character-defining features' of an area to be clearly
identified. It must be stressed, however, that while a landscape can be disaggregated
into a series of discrete components (or themes: see work currently underway in Wales
in Part Two) these were all functionally interrelated:

20

- **settlement pattern**: where people live and work, and where goods (transported through the communication system) are created and consumed.

- **communication networks**: both man-made, such as roads and canals, and the use of natural features such as rivers, estuaries, and the sea. The means by which agricultural goods, extracted minerals and manufactured products are transported from source to final destination (usually elements of the settlement pattern, but sometimes different elements of the fieldscape). In the past roads and droveways formed a continuation of common land (see unenclosed land below).

- **field systems**: mostly used for arable, pasture, and meadow, though lattorly also specialised horticulture. Patterns of landuse are determined by both the natural environment (eg climate, soils, relief) and cultural factors such as tenurial structures and proximity to centres of consumption. The character of field systems will reflect partly the agricultural practices of the period from which they originate and partly subsequent changes in landuse, such as long narrow fields with a reversed-S plan that are derived from the piecemeal enclosure of arable open fields whose survival until today is the result of a change in landuse to pasture which meant they escaped the large-scale removal of field boundaries associated with the 20th-century mechanisation of arable farming (eg Johnson 1996, fig 3.5).

- **woodland**: an important managed resource long before the proliferation of conifer plantations. Source of fuel (including charcoal) and building materials, which needed to be transported to settlements and industrial sites. Could form part of other landscape components such as medieval deer parks, or post-medieval landscaped parkland.

- **unenclosed land**: often referred to as common or 'waste', though the latter is an unfortunate term as it fails to recognise its economic importance for grazing etc. Today mostly found in intertidal and upland areas, though some areas of lowland common still survives (eg roadside waste and village greens which were far more significant in the past, often being the focus of settlement). Roads and droveways often had funnel-shaped entrances where they entered a common to facilitate the movement of livestock (eg Figs 1, 13.4, and 15.4).

- **industrial complexes**: extractive and manufacturing, ranging from large-scale industrial landscapes, to smaller-scale activity scattered throughout the wider rural/urban landscapes (eg Figs 8–9, and 11). Specialised industrial landscapes will contain other components such as transport infrastructure and settlements for the industrial workers (differing in character to those rural settlements where agricultural employment has traditionally predominated).

- **open water**: before their drainage, natural areas of open water formed an important part of some landscapes being valued for fishing and wildfowling (eg Meare case study in Part Three; and see Bond 1988, 80–1; Coney 1992; Hall 1992, 30–3; Lucas 1998). The management of water within designed landscapes has a long history with the earliest artificial reservoirs and fishponds dating to the Roman period (Zeepvat 1988; McOmish *et al* 2002), and water supply and fishpond complexes being an important feature of many medieval high-status sites (eg Hadleigh case study below, Fig 15.4; and see Aston 1988a; Bond 1989; 2001). Modern reservoirs are, however, on an altogether different scale.

* **military facilities**: defensive features can be scattered throughout the rural/ urban landscape (eg lines of pill boxes), or concentrated into discrete military facilities (eg Second World War airfields). The division between military and civilian is not always that clear cut; the Roman frontiers in northern Britain – whose impressive remains form relict landscapes which still dominate the historic landscape character of these areas – would have served an important role in controlling the movement of people and livestock, and a number of forts saw the development of civilian *vicus* settlements (Woodside and Crow 1999).

* **recreation**: some landscapes are devoted to leisure (such as marinas, seafronts, and piers at coastal resorts), while sometimes recreation was just one aspect of a multi-faceted landscape (eg medieval deer parks, which were also important sources of food, timber and underwood).

Other influences on the historic character of the countryside are more conceptual in nature:

* **patterns of exchange, trade, and consumption**: most notably towns, but also places such as military establishments, would have drawn in rural resources such as food and material used in manufacturing, and were usually the means for articulating the distribution of industrial products (in the medieval period rural fairs were also important though they have usually left little or no trace in the historic landscape). As such, towns would have had a profound effect on the transport infrastructure and local landuse, promoting the emergence of regional economies (eg Everitt 1979; Campbell *et al* 1993).

* **status and power**: wealth and power are derived from the control of land and communities, and this is reflected in the landscape. It is increasingly recognised, for example, that sites such as medieval castles were as much symbols of status and power as simply military installations (Liddiard 2000; Creighton 2002). A castle would often form part of a wider *seigniorial landscape*, reflecting the power and authority of an aristocratic elite, illustrated for example by deer parks and fishponds (eg see Hadleigh case study below).

* **designed/ornamental landscapes**: from the Neolithic, complexes of ritual monuments show that space was being structured and manipulated in a planned fashion, sometimes with reference to features in the natural landscape (Tilley 1995; 1996). In more recent times, designed parks and gardens are predominantly a post-medieval phenomenon, but there is increasing evidence for landscape design in the medieval period from at least the 12th century, associated with both castles (eg Everson *et al* 2000; Liddiard 2000; Creighton 2002) and other high status residences (Taylor 1989a; Landsberg 1996; Oosthuizen and Taylor 2000). The use of water was a common feature (Everson 1996a; b; 1998; Taylor 2000). In part such

Figure 10: Painting by Henry Bright c 1845 of the ruined south-east tower of Hadleigh Castle, with St Clement's parish church Leigh-on-Sea in the background, overlooking the Thames Estuary in Essex (© Southend-on-Sea Museum). The church, rebuilt in the 15th century, and castle, occupied between the 1230s and 1550s, were both in use at the same time, but only the church still forms a functioning part of the historic landscape; the 'relict' castle, however, still dominates the Thames and forms an important part of the historic landscape character of today (and see Fig 15.4). This is also an example of how certain evocative locations can assume great cultural/historical significance through the work of writers and painters. In the case of Hadleigh local mythology, written down in the legend of the white wizard or 'cunning man', Cunning Murrell, suggests the castle is haunted and is an ancient smugglers den, reflecting the strong maritime links of this area (Morrison 1900)

landscapes were concerned with leisure, but they were also great statements of power and played an important part in social discourse.

- **tenurial structure**: the pattern of estates and landholding that provided the social context within which landscapes originated and evolved. Individuals, institutions and communities could take decisions that shaped the character of settlement patterns and field systems both in the long term (eg the communal/ customary management of an open field, or regulation of grazing on an area of common), and the short term (eg the passing of an Act of Enclosure). This is explored in the case studies of Hadleigh (Fig 15), the Caldicot Level (Figs 17 and 20), Meare (Fig 28) and Somerset (Fig 27).

- **a sense of place/belonging**: the symbolic/ritual value of places, both natural and man-made, and other cultural associations, for example with writers and painters (eg Fig 10). Important to both residents and visitors/tourists in terms of how they perceive the character of a landscape.

Historic landscape types, zones, and areas

Whilst the historic landscape of an area can be disaggregated into its different components, the overall character of a particular place results from the way in which all the components articulate with each other. Certain repetitive combinations give rise to a series of *generic* historic landscape **types**. In some cases these types are relatively simple and contain relatively few components (eg ancient woodland, modern plantations, quarries etc), but agrarian landscapes in particular can be complex. Two examples show the contrast (note that there is a clear distinction between objective description, and the inferred process that led to the creation of each landscape type in a particular period):

- Large areas of carefully laid out large, rectilinear fields (with names usually ending in Acre), containing the occasional 18th-century farm, surrounding a nucleated village with a range of farmsteads including medieval buildings, from which radiate a series of long straight roads with no waste: Parliamentary Enclosure of former open fields.
- A complex pattern of small, irregular-shaped fields (with a great diversity of names including 'breach'), associated with a series of isolated farmsteads and small hamlets all containing medieval and post-medieval buildings, and linked by winding lanes with small areas of common/roadside waste: medieval woodland assarting.

When analysing the historic landscape care should be taken to identify not only blocks of countryside of a coherent type, but also landscape elements that might mark significant boundaries that either form part of the structure of that type (eg a series of long axial field boundaries laid out during enclosure, around which the former common or open field was divided up into fields), or its boundary (eg a 'head dike' marking the upslope limit of a field system in an upland area).

In some cases, landscape of a particular **type** may occur over a relatively large area, while elsewhere its extent may be very limited such that a large number of types can be distinguished in a particular locale. In these cases a particular combination of types can be generalised or simplified into a series of generic **zones** where the recurrent association of certain historic landscape character types reflect common patterns of development. The identification of zones in this way was pioneered in the Cornwall Historic Landscape Characterisation (see Colour Plate A, and Part Three) but has not been widely adopted since, though it remains a potentially useful approach where there is considerable complexity.

At a broader level, distinctive **historic landscape character areas** can then be distinguished on the basis of their unique combination of inter-related components, types, and zones. The recognition of such character areas sometimes has a long pedigree. In c1540, for example, John Leland wrote of the two major character areas in Warwickshire:

> I learnt [at Warwick] that the most part of the shire of Warwickshire, that lies as the river Avon descends on the right hand of it, is in Arden (for so in ancient name of that part of the shire) and the ground in Arden is muche enclosed, plentiful of grass, but no great plenty of corne...The other part of Warwickshire that lies on the left hand of the Avon river, muche to the south is for the most part champion [open field], somewhat barren of wood, but very plentiful of corn. (based on Toulmin Smith 1908, 47).

The Arden region of Warwickshire was also relatively well wooded, while the 'champion' district, also known as the 'Felden', was part of what is now recognised as England's 'Central Province' characterised by open fields and nucleated villages (Ford 1979; Everitt 1985, 3–4; Roberts 1987, 170–2; Hooke 1993; 1998, 144–50, 161–3; Watkins 1993; Roberts and Wrathmell 2000a, fig 20; 2000b). Understanding fundamental regional differences in historic landscape character is a key theme in this handbook.

The level of detailed resolution achieved in defining types, zones, and areas will depend on the nature of the research being undertaken, and the time and resources available. In a detailed parish study it may be possible to have a series of very precisely defined types (ie highly homogeneous) whose extent in some cases may be relatively limited (eg a small block of fields covering a few hectares: see Meare case study in Part Three for which the base map was the First Edition Ordnance Survey Six Inch to the mile maps of approximately 1:10,560 scale). The resulting simplified zones/character areas may similarly only cover a relatively small area. In larger-scale projects, where large areas have to be analysed more quickly, some of the types and zones may be defined more broadly (ie allowing for slightly less homogeneity) and so end up covering rather larger areas of several sq km. In the county-scale English Heritage sponsored Historic Landscape Characterisation Projects modern base maps of 1:25,000 scale are generally used.

Approaching the task: top-down or bottom-up

There are broadly two approaches to identifying historic landscape character areas. The **bottom-up approach** starts with a base map showing all the landscape components (ie a minimum scale of 1:25,000 that shows all individual fields). Each of these land parcels is then ascribed to one of a number of predetermined generic landscape types; adjacent parcels with the same characteristics will be attributed to the same type leading to the identification of parts of the landscape with the same historic character. This can be done on computer (using a Geographical Information Systems (GIS) package) or on paper copy by literally colouring in each parcel/field. Another approach is to label or 'tag' each parcel with a number of attributes (size, shape, date etc) though this can only be carried out using a GIS. Once every field etc is labelled in some way, the data can be simplified by identifying zones and ultimately areas.

This 'bottom-up' approach is systematic and objective, but can be time-consuming. For an experienced researcher a quicker, subjective approach is to work from the **top-down** identifying the major divisions in landscape character through professional judgement (based on prior knowledge or a rapid assessment of landscape character). This entails simply drawing a line around a block of landscape of relatively coherent character (see discussion of work in Wales in Part Three).

The colour, texture, language, and experience of landscape

So far discussion has focused on aspects of the historic landscape that can be classified on the basis of their appearance on maps. 'Landscape', however, is not just culturally constructed in a physical sense: its *perceived* character will vary depending on how it is viewed. While field boundary patterns may be one of the most extensive components to analyse using maps and air photographs, in practice they may not be the most significant factor in how communities experience their countryside *on the ground*. In an anciently enclosed landscape, the winding lanes and scattered settlements are just as important, and actually more evident on the ground, compared to the small irregular-shaped fields that cover by far the greatest area. In fact, for many drivers, familiar with different regions of Britain, the daily perception of a landscape might be more influenced by the experience of constant braking to drive around a bend or avoid mud on the road as one passes yet another dairy farm, rather than the shape of the fields hidden behind a hedge (say in Devon/Cornwall). Such an experience would contrast sharply with the straight and open roads of the Midlands.

Another visual aspect of historic landscape character is that of its colour, texture, and materials. A key feature of the mid-Devon landscape, for example, is its red soils, so different to the white chalky soils of nearby Wessex. Geology is also a significant determinant in the physical form taken by field boundaries which range from neat drystone walls and earthen banks to hedgerows or ditches. Geology is also one influence on vernacular architecture, most notably on the balance between stone, timber, and cob (clay, gravel, and straw) in walls, and thatch, slate, and tiles on roofs. Such distinctive variations can occur across broad regions, such as the elaborate pargeting (decorative moulded plasterwork painted in light pastel colours) on timber-framed houses in East Anglia, that contrasts with the weatherboarding that is common in the Home Counties (Brunskill 1992). In places, the colour and texture that geology gives to vernacular architecture is more subtle, such as the contrasting orange (Ham Stone) and blue-grey (Lias) limestones in central and southern Somerset, the red stone/cob of mid-Devon, and granite of the South West's moorlands. Elsewhere variations in vernacular architecture result from socio-economic factors such as top-floor 'weavers windows' reflecting the importance of the cloth industry in the North West. Even the design of buildings shows marked regional variation: in south-east England, late medieval houses were of the 'Wealden House' type, with a central hall open to the roof, between two-storey blocks with projecting first-floor jetties either side, whereas in the South West, longhouses were the dominant form, with a kitchen/living room and inner private room to one side of a cross-passage and a service room/cow house to the other (reflecting the strongly pastoral economy of this region) (Brunskill 1992).

26

Figure 11: Wheal Betsy, Mary Mavy on the western fringes of Dartmoor, Devon. This ancient silver-lead mine was reopened in 1806 and was water-powered until the present wheelhouse was built to house a cornish beam pump engine. The surrounding landscape is covered by extensive remains of mining and quarrying to the extent that the historic landscape character of this area would be 'relict industrial/mining' (photo: the author)

The language of the landscape also contributes to its character, such as the 'dales' of Yorkshire, and the 'dens' of the Weald, and the sudden change from farmsteads with English '-ton' and '-cott' place-names to the Cornish 'Tre-' almost immediately one crosses the River Tamar (Padel 1999). In parts of the east and north, Scandinavian place-name elements add local distinctiveness. In many regions discrete clusters of '-leigh' names characterise settlements in more wooded areas (eg the Arden district of Warwickshire: see above), while in north-west England place-names ending in '-shaw' (eg Ollerenshaw in Derbyshire) are a distinct regional variant (Gelling and Cole 2000, 245–6). The remote character of many valleys in three other discrete upland regions – the central Welsh Marches, the southern/eastern Pennines, and the mountainous areas of western County Durham, Northumbria and southern Scotland – is marked by concentrations of place-names with the Old English *hop* element (eg Hopesay and Ratlinghope in Shropshire: Gelling and Cole 2000, 133–40); in the hillier parts of the South West, Wessex, and the Cotswolds 'combe' place-names similarly refer to settled valleys, while in the South East the more common term is '-den'/'-dean'. The 'hope' place-name element also reflects the remoteness of the coastal marshes in south-east England, where it is used in the sense of 'enclosure in marsh' alongside a range of other distinctive place-name elements, such as '-wick' and '-worth', which add to the special character of these landscapes (Rippon 2000a). Further local distinctiveness is brought about through even more subtle variations in the language of landscape, such

27

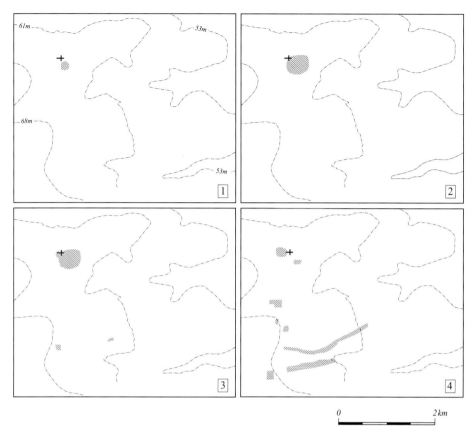

Figure 12: Longham, Norfolk. When interpreting the results of archaeological survey and excavation of buried/relict medieval landscapes it is essential to integrate that evidence with those parts of the medieval landscape that remain in use today. 1–4: pottery scatters cannot be understood without reference to the wider fabric of the landscape. 1: 'Middle Saxon' Ipswich Ware (mid-7th to mid-9th century); 2: 'Late Saxon' Thetford Ware (mid-9th to late 12th century); 3: 'Early Medieval Ware' (late 11th to 12th century); 4: 'Grimston Ware' (13th to 14th century) (Wade-Martins 1980, 5–6);

as the term for an artificial watercourse varying between 'rhyne' in Somerset, 'rhine' in Gloucestershire and 'reen' in Wales; in Romney Marsh the same features are called 'sewers', while in Fenland the term 'lode' was common (Rippon 1997a; 2000a). There are also regionally distinctive field-names, such as 'park' (enclosed field) and 'gratton' (stubble, ie cultivated field), 'cleave' (steep slope) and 'down' (upland pasture) in the South West (eg Fig 19), all of which adds to the distinctive character of these local landscapes and can be an important part of historic landscape analysis through linking historical references to landscape features with the physical fabric of the landscape itself (eg Meare case study: Part Three).

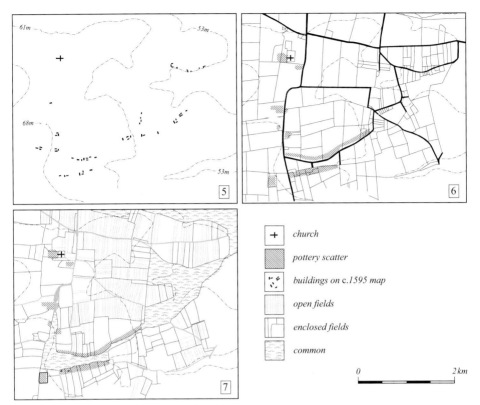

Figure 12 (continued) 5: buildings shown on an undated estate map of c 1595; 6: 13th- to 14th-century settlement in relation to the modern landscape: a relationship to the road pattern becomes clear, though the main area of occupation in the south is curiously set back from the road; 7: all becomes clear: 13th- to 14th-century settlement in relation to the landscape as depicted on a map of c 1595: the main area of occupation lay adjacent to an area of common (after Wade-Martins 1980, figs 14–16; (re-drawn by Mike Rouillard)

Relict and historic landscapes

So far discussion has focused on how historic landscape analysis highlights the time-depth present in the character of the present, *still-functioning* countryside. What distinguishes this *historic landscape* from other aspects of the archaeological record is that it is principally concerned with features that are still in use today, in contrast to abandoned – or *relict* – elements of earlier stages of landscape development that survive above ground as earthworks or ruins (eg Figs 10 and 11). Other landscapes have been completely *buried* by later deposits, as in floodplains and other wetlands, or ploughed flat where they are only revealed as cropmarks or through fieldwalking. The scatters of material revealed through fieldwalking may predate, and so be completely unrelated to, the present landscape, though deserted or shrunken medieval settlements are simply parts of the historic landscape that have been abandoned and so can only be understood when mapped alongside those aspects of the medieval landscape that continued in use long enough to appear on post-medieval cartographic sources or even survive in use today (eg Fig 12; and see Silvester 1988; 1993).

Relict remains can, however, make a significant contribution to the character of the historic landscape, and to understanding long-term change in the countryside (ie how the present historic landscape came into being). The earthworks of a bank and ditch, or even a line of trees running across an arable field, are suggestive of an old field boundary that was formerly part of the historic landscape. In other cases whole components of a past landscape have been abandoned, but although no longer performing their original function their remains still form part of the character of the countryside today. Sometimes these remains only survive as an individual site, but where such features are fairly extensive, and retain sufficient coherence, they can be regarded as 'relict landscapes' (eg Fig 11). Elsewhere, such relict remains are set within the context of a still-living 'historic landscape', such as the waste tips from abandoned slate quarries that tower above many working villages in north Wales (Gwyn 2001). In other cases the relict remains are more slight but still make a significant contribution to historic landscape character, such as the earthworks/tumbled stone walls of abandoned prehistoric, Romano-British and medieval field systems that are spread across many of our western islands (eg Skomer: Evans 1990; St Kilda: Fleming 2001) and upland fringes (eg Bodmin Moor: Johnson and Rose 1994; the Cheviot Hills: C Campbell *et al* 2002; Dartmoor: Fig 13; Fleming 1988; Gerrard 1997; north Wales: Silvester 2000; Salisbury Plain: Bradley *et al* 1994; McOmish *et al* 2002; Yorkshire Dales: Horne and MacLeod 2001). These relict field boundaries may not in themselves be that impressive but they are often picked out by different types of vegetation, which along with shadow, adds visual texture and graining to these landscapes. In some cases long abandoned field boundaries appear to have been reused when areas were recolonised in the medieval period (eg parts of the Dartmoor Reaves: Fig 13; Fleming 1988, figs 15, 31 and 69; St David's Head, Pembrokeshire: Murphy 2001), and in a very few cases it is possible to postulate that prehistoric and Romano-British field systems have remained in continuous use and form the basis of the modern historic landscape (eg East Anglian Boulder Clays: Williamson 1987, 1998; south-east Essex: Rippon 1991; West Penwith, Cornwall: Herring 1993; *cf* Hinton 1997).

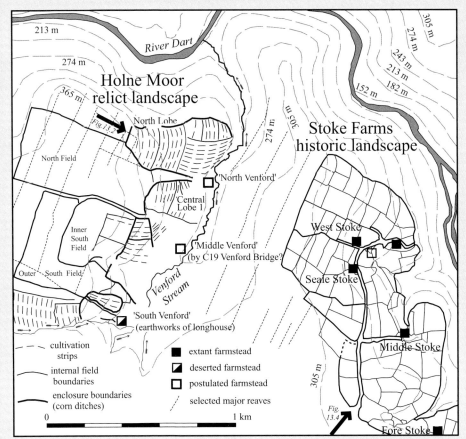

Figure 13.1: Holne Moor, Dartmoor, Devon. A medieval 'relict landscape' on the western slopes of the Venford Stream, and extant 'historic landscape' at Stoke (after Fleming and Ralph 1982, fig 3 and plate III; Devon SMR SX67SE-243, 380; Ordnance Survey First Edition Six Inch Map, Devon Sheet 107 SW; air photographs: NMR SX6970/1/299, SX6971/1/61, SX6871 1457/470-2) (drawing: the author)

CASE STUDY: HOLNE MOOR, DARTMOOR *(FIG 13)*

Key features

- *Case study showing how elements of the archaeological record can comprise parts of the historic landscape that have gone out of use*
- *Such deserted landscapes can show us what adjacent areas of historic landscape would have looked like during the medieval period*

Fleming and Ralph's (1982) survey and interpretation of the medieval relict landscape on Holne Moor, Dartmoor, was a classic piece of landscape archaeology though it predated the concept of the 'historic landscape'. It was mapped as a piece of

Figure 13.2: The 'North Lobe' of the Holne Moor relict landscape, overlying an element of an earlier relict landscape: the middle Bronze Age reave system (in the foreground). The north-south oriented cultivation strips in the north-eastern sector of the North Lobe can be seen in the distance (photo: the author)

'archaeology', but the remains on Holne Moor can actually be thought of as part of the historic landscape that has simply gone out of use (the well known deserted medieval settlement at Hound Tor is similarly an abandoned part of a still-used medieval landscape: Austin and Walker 1985).

The medieval relict landscape on the western slopes of the Venford Stream comprises a series of abandoned field systems with earlier lobe-shaped enclosures on the valley sides, subdivided into cultivation strips defined by low banks, with larger, rectilinear fields upslope (Figs 13.1–2). Note how these relict remains form a significant part of the colour and texture of the historic landscape which would otherwise be regarded simply as an 'unenclosed upland pasture' type. The southern-most lobe is associated with a deserted farmstead ('South Venford' on Fig 13.1) and a series of droveways, with funnel-shaped entrances leading down from the open moor, suggest other deserted settlements are now under forestry and the Venford Reservoir ('Middle' and 'North' Venford on Fig 13.1).

The Holne Moor relict medieval landscape overlies an earlier, Bronze Age relict field system known as the 'reaves' (Fig 13.1–2). The early lobe-shaped enclosures ignored these relatively slight remains, though the later fields upslope reused certain reaves, resulting in a more rectilinear layout. The historic landscape at Seale Stoke and West Stoke similarly reuses some of the reaves.

On the opposite side of the Venford Valley lie a series of isolated farms with the place-name 'Stoke', and their associated field systems (Fig 13.3). The field boundary patterns here are, at first sight, rather different to the relict landscape on Holne Moor:

Figure 13.3: Fields north of West Stoke, looking west from Aish Tor, across the Dart Valley. The landscape of the Stoke Farms probably looks similar to what Holne Moor might have been had it not been abandoned (photo: the author)

the fields and enclosures at Holne Moor appear larger than those at Stoke which might lead one to conclude that these two landscapes are of different date. In fact these landscapes were occupied at the same time as Stoke is documented in Domesday (Glover *et al* 1931, 302), and the lobe-shaped enclosures at Holne Moor are 12th-century or earlier (Fleming and Ralph 1982, 105–9). The different layout of these two landscapes results from the fact that at Holne Moor landscape development was halted, whereas at Stoke the landscape has continued to evolve through to the present day. In the 12th century Stoke probably had a layout similar to that on Holne Moor, and Holne Moor would probably have looked like Stoke had it not been abandoned. A good example is the relict funnel-shaped droveway west of 'North Venford' that would have looked like the extant example leading from Holne Lee Moor to the Stoke Farms (Fig 13.4; see Fig 13.1 for its location). Note that areas of roadside waste such as this have usually been enclosed, leading to a straight narrow road with distinctive long, thin fields on either side (eg see Fig 1). The stone-revetted earthen banks topped with hedges form another distinctive part of this historic landscape.

It is also noticeable how the cultivation strips in the Holne Moor lobes curve off to the left, as do a number of the extant field boundaries to the north of West Stoke, a feature of the historic landscape that is seen elsewhere in the upland fringes of south-west England including Bodmin Moor and Exmoor (Johnson and Rose 1994, 100–15; Pattison 1999; Riley and Wilson-North 2001, 98–102; Gillard 2002; and see Fig 18). It could be argued that north of West Stoke the extant field boundaries were created to enclose what had been a small open field (like the north lobe on Holne Moor), and that the present boundaries simply followed earlier cultivation strips (in the same way that reversed-S shaped fields were sometimes produced from the piecemeal 'enclosure by

Figure 13.4: Funnel-shaped droveway leading from Holne Lee Moor to the Stoke Farms. Areas of roadside waste such as this have usually been enclosed, leading to a straight narrow road with distinctive long, thin fields on either side (see Fig 15.2). The distinctive stone-revetted earthen banks, topped with hedges form a distinctive part of this historic landscape (photo: the author)

agreement' of Midland open fields). Elsewhere the old cultivation strips appear to have been swept away and an entirely new field system imposed which is why the landscape of today is at first sight so dissimilar.

Putting people in the landscape: the concept of 'natural beauty' and the role of the natural environment in shaping historic landscape character

So far, discussion has focused on our cultural landscape: fields, roads, settlements etc. This contrasts with the popular perception of landscape and major pieces of planning legislation which are concerned with concepts such as 'Sites of Special Scientific Interest' and 'Areas of Outstanding Natural Beauty'. The idea of 'natural beauty' is itself a cultural construct and a very misleading one that does a major disservice to the human communities who have created and still maintain the countryside of today. Even most ecological 'Sites of Special Scientific Interest' have little to do with things 'natural' and a lot to do with things cultural: flower-rich meadows, for example, are the product of careful land management and the annual cutting of hay, while bracken, gorse, and heather-covered moorland results from woodland clearance, soil depletion, different

Figure 14: Teignhead Farm on Dartmoor: the abandonment of farms on the high moor facilitated the creation of this 'wilderness' area in the 20th century (photo: the author)

livestock grazing regimes, and periodic deliberate burning to control the vegetation. One might think that an upland area like Dartmoor, for example, is a 'natural' landscape but this is far from the case: woodland has been cleared, large areas were once bogs, with some areas then recolonised in the medieval period (Fig 13.1). In part the current 'wilderness' appearance of central Dartmoor is the product of early human exploitation of the environment, and in part settlement desertion as late as the 20th century (Fig 14).

Understanding the past is essential for managing the future, and some progress has been made in persuading countryside managers of this. Throughout the 1990s the Countryside Agency (and its predecessor the Countryside Commission) developed a methodology for 'Landscape Character Assessment'. Although recognising cultural factors such as settlement and historical perceptions, the early examples of LCA tended to place the greatest emphasis on visual appearance – physical landscape (landform) and habitat types (landcover) – with only limited recognition of the significance and complexity of the time-depth present (Countryside Commission 1993; eg Warwickshire; Countryside Commission 1991; *cf* Chichester Harbour: Countryside Commission 1992; Hooke 1993). In 1994 the publication of *Views from the Past: Historic Landscape Character in the English Countryside* marked an important step forward in recognising the cultural contribution to landscape character (Countryside Commission 1994a), though in the same year the Countryside Commission embarked upon its *New Map of England* project to map landscape character across England, starting with a pilot study in the South West (Countryside Commission 1994c). The character areas were, however, essentially based on geology, topography, and present appearance of the countryside with only limited acknowledgement of cultural processes that contributed to the 'evolution of the landscape'. The final map of *The Character of England: landscape, wildlife and natural features* regressed even further down this 'landscape as natural beauty' avenue in combining these 'Character Areas' with English Nature's 'Natural Areas' (Countryside Commission and English Nature 1996).

It was similarly disappointing to see that the Countryside Agency and Scottish Natural Heritage's *Landscape Character Assessment Guidance* was drawn up by a firm of landscape architects and a university 'Department of Landscape' without a significant contribution from those with a clear understanding of the historical processes that have led to the landscape's current appearance. The report acknowledges that 'to understand the "time-depth" aspects of landscape requires expert analysis' so it is perhaps surprising that such 'experts' were not involved in preparing those guidelines (Swanwick *et al.* 1999; http://www.countryside.gov.uk/cci/ guidance.htm). In the initial information gathering stage, for example, the need to consult any existing historic landscape work is not even mentioned, and in the initial mapping stage, 'Where resources are limited and time is short, the desk study may need to be limited to an assessment of geology, landform, land cover and settlement distribution. In these cases the opportunity should be taken to update and amplify the data collected, especially in terms of the historic dimension, *when time and resources become available*' (italics added). The statement that 'Patterns of field enclosure can be interpreted from 1:25,000 OS data and from aerial photographs, again using land cover analysis. Map analysis, however, *only provides an understanding of the contemporary patterns* of settlement and enclosure without the important "time-depth" dimension of their historical origins' (italics added) is an astonishing assertion that is simply incorrect. The historic landscape as mapped in two dimensions provides abundant information on time-depth as some fifty years of academic research since Hoskins, the ongoing programme of HLC/HLA, and hopefully this handbook have shown. Whilst there are examples of collaboration at the local level (eg the Bath and north-east Somerset LCA: 2003), archaeologists, historians and historical geographers clearly still have some way to go in persuading the 'natural environment' agencies that the 'cultural environment' is an equal partner and that it is impossible to understand and manage the landscape without a more integrated approach.

The influence that the natural environment (geology, topography, climate, ecosystems etc) has had on how the cultural character of the countryside has evolved is much debated and a detailed discussion is beyond the scope of this handbook. Suffice to say that until the 1990s archaeologists and historical geographers had moved away from the traditional idea (eg Fox 1932) that the natural structure of the environment determined how human society evolved. There has, however, been some revisionist debate in recent years and a recognition that the fear of being labelled 'geographical deterministic' means that scholars may have been reluctant to give due consideration to the potential role of the natural environment in shaping cultural landscapes (Muir 1999, 112–13; Tipping 2002). Butlin and Roberts (1995, 10), for example, have suggested that 'recent ideas in cultural geography, which emphasise the significance of the cultural construction of landscapes by human imagination and agency, are now being questioned in relation to their apparent underestimation of the role of the physical environments in people-environmental relationships'. McGlade (1999) has similarly argued that the pendulum has swung too far in the direction of a wholly humanist approach and that the natural environment provides the crucial context within which human cultures created landscapes (and see Coones 1985; Corcos 2002, 190): the analysis of place-names certainly demonstrates an acute awareness in the past of subtle but significant differences in the physical characteristics of the environment (Gelling and Cole 2000, xvii). Williamson's (2003) stimulating discussion of the origins of open field farming has progressed this debate even further in arguing for a link between the character of soils and the development of common field agriculture in the East Midlands/East Anglia. It should also be remembered that the physical character of the landscape can change: soils can be eroded following woodland clearance and arable cultivation, or leached of their nutrients, become waterlogged, acidic and even buried beneath peat. Human intervention can equally improve the condition of soils through marling, manuring, and under drainage. Changing technology can make farming easier in areas that were previously difficult, or mineral deposits that were previously inaccessible available to be exploited.

Analysis of the historic landscape shows that the natural environment certainly did have a profound effect on the character of our countryside, but that ultimately it was human agency that determined the form that this took. The history of reclaimed coastal marshes around Britain, for example, reveals how during the medieval period most coastal marshes were embanked and drained, but that in some areas, such as the Thames Estuary, physically identical saltmarshes were left unreclaimed because the profits of dairy production close to a major urban centre (eg London) were equal or greater to that from farming a reclaimed marsh. The same type of environment could have a variety of cultural landscapes due to a range of socio-economic factors and the nature of landownership (Rippon 2000a, 229–40; and see Hadleigh case study below, and Caldicot Level case study in Part Two). When putting 'people back in the landscape' one must also not forget the role of both individuals and communities. The contribution of the great post-medieval landowners and the landscape designers they employed is clear. However, just who did decide to create the great open fields and who planned the villages of the Midlands – lords or the community – is still debated (eg Dyer 1985; Harvey 1989). The impact of different patterns of landowning on landscape character is explored further in the case studies of Hadleigh in Part One, and Somerset in Part Three.

CASE STUDY: HADLEIGH, ESSEX *(FIG 15)*

Key features:

- *multi-period parish-scale case study*
- *simple demonstration of how the historic landscape comprises a set of articulated components which taken together define the key character defining features of different areas*
- *a 'past-oriented' analysis forming part of wider research into landscape history through integrating a variety of sources (including field archaeology, documentary/ cartographic material, and place-names)*
- *demonstrates how different historic landscape character results from different processes of landscape creation and evolution, and the various social structures behind them*
- *further reading:* Rippon 1999a.

Introduction

The following simple case study is designed to illustrate some of the key issues introduced so far, notably how a historic landscape can be broken down into its elements/ parcels, components, types and areas. For the sake of brevity and coherence, attention will focus on the period between the 13th and 19th centuries. The example chosen here is the parish of Hadleigh in south-east Essex (see Rippon 1991 and 1999a, and Wymer and Brown 1995, 151–73 for background to the region). In terms of the physical topography and soils, the landscape can be divided into four (Fig 15.1):

- an extensive area of flat, estuarine alluvium derived from saltmarshes and mudflats in the south
- a series of hills and valleys (the southern hills) rising above the marshes with soils mostly derived from sands and gravels
- a relatively flat central plateau, with soils derived from sands and gravels with heavier gravelly loam and clay ('head') on the lower slopes
- the Prittle Brook Valley in the north with loamy soils (derived from 'head').

Sources

The base map used to interrogate the historic landscape is the First Edition Ordnance Survey Six Inch Map surveyed in 1867 (Fig 15.2). Use is also made of the Tithe Survey[1] that maps the whole parish in 1847, the county map of Chapman and André of 1777, and five other maps cover small parts of the parish: namely the Enclosure map of 1852 (which covers the former common),[2] estate maps of the lands of the Dean and Chapter of St Paul's Cathedral (1750)[3] and Sayers Farm (1709),[4] and maps of Hadleigh Park (undated, but probably 17th century) and the 'Mill and Hadley Park Marshes' (1670) before they were enclosed and drained[5] (Fig 15.3).

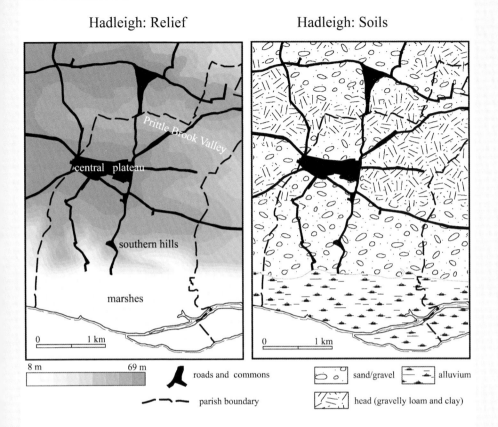

Hadleigh: Relief

Hadleigh: Soils

Prittle Brook Valley

central plateau

southern hills

marshes

| 0 | 1 km |

| 0 | 1 km |

| 8 m | 69 m |

roads and commons

- - - parish boundary

sand/gravel

alluvium

head (gravelly loam and clay)

Figure 15.1: Hadleigh, Essex: relief and soils (drawing: the author)

Historic landscape components

settlement pattern (Fig 15.4):
- a small nucleated village on the southern side of the common and adjacent to the church and manor (Hadleigh Hall)
- settlements scattered elsewhere around the common, including Solby's and Common Hall Farms and more recent non-agrarian buildings (the Rectory, Workhouse, and Turnpike Cottage)
- isolated farmsteads scattered across the rest of the parish but linked to the Common by droveways (Sayers Farm, Castle Farm, Park Farm, Bramble Hall, and Garrold's Farm).

communication networks (Fig 15.4):
- a series of roads/droveways radiate from the common linking it with the marshes, outlying farms, and the wider world

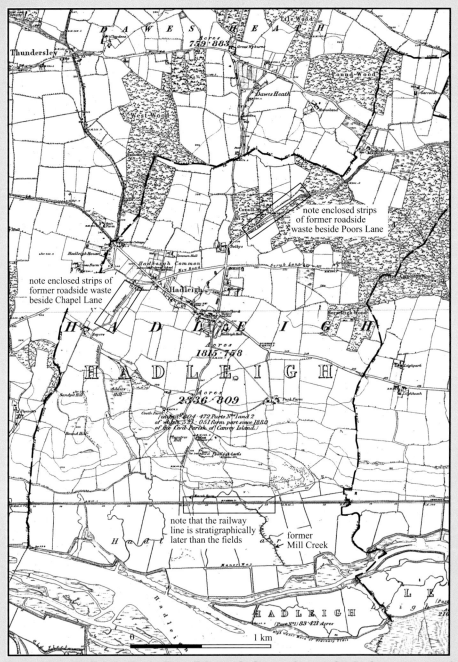

Figure 15.2: Hadleigh, Essex: First Edition Ordnance Survey Six Inch map surveyed in 1867. Note the strips of enclosed roadside waste when the Chapel Lane and Poors Lane droveways were enclosed (cf Fig 15.3) (drawing: the author)

Tithe Map: 1847

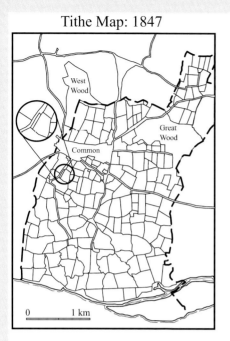

West Wood

Great Wood

Common

0   1 km

Chapman and André: 1777

17th-18th century estate maps

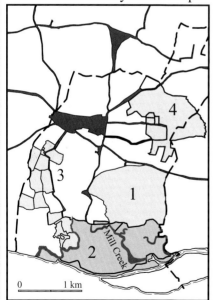

4

3

1

Mill Creek

2

0   1 km

 creek

1. ?17th century: Hadley Park

2. 1670: Mill Marsh and Hadley Mill Marsh

3. 1709: Sayers Farm

4: 1750: Dean and Chapter of St Paul's
(Great Wood and Scrub House)

Figure 15.3: Hadleigh, Essex: Tithe Map of 1847, extract from Chapman and André's county map of 1777, and those parts of Hadleigh depicted on earlier estate maps. Note the enclosed roadside waste beside Chapel Lane (drawing: the author)

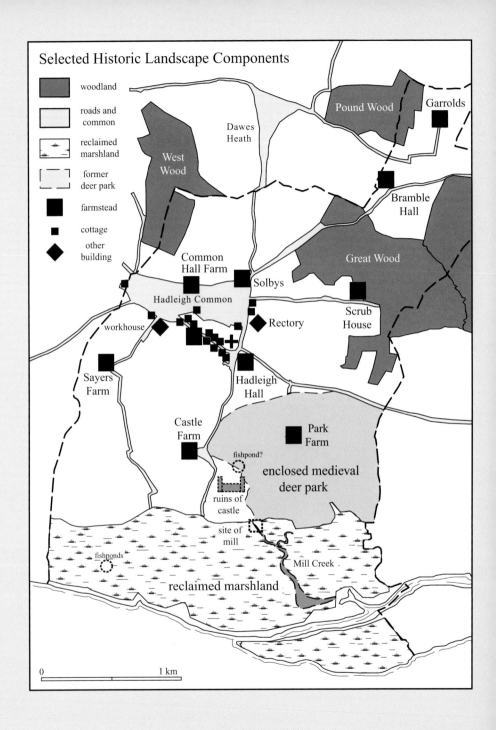

Selected Historic Landscape Components

woodland

roads and common

reclaimed marshland

former deer park

farmstead

cottage

other building

Pound Wood

Garrolds

Dawes Heath

West Wood

Bramble Hall

Great Wood

Common Hall Farm

Solbys

Hadleigh Common

Rectory

Scrub House

workhouse

Sayers Farm

Hadleigh Hall

Castle Farm

Park Farm

fishpond?

enclosed medieval deer park

ruins of castle

site of mill

Mill Creek

fishponds

reclaimed marshland

0   1 km

42

- the mid-19th-century railway cuts uncomfortably across the reclaimed marshes (where it is clearly stratigraphically later than the field boundary pattern: Fig 15.2)
- 'Mill Creek', shown on the map of 1670, but largely silted up by 1777 (when it is shown as a relict feature: Fig 15.3). A buried vessel laden with building stone, discovered when the railway line was constructed, shows that shipping used the creek (Rippon 1999a).

field boundary patterns (Fig 15.5):

Comparison of the various cartographic sources reveals the date and processes whereby several of the field boundary patterns were created:
- Park Farm: medium–large broadly rectilinear fields created after the conversion of the former deer park to agricultural use during/after the 17th century. The line of the former park pale still survives as a field boundary enclosing this block of fields
- Hadleigh Marshes: large, highly irregular-shaped fields resulting from the drainage of former saltmarshes after 1670, with the meandering courses of old tidal creeks sometimes being used as field boundaries
- Broom Wood and 'TM 145-6, 148-9':[6] large rectangular fields postdating woodland clearance after 1777
- Hadleigh Common: straight-sided polygonal fields created by Parliamentary Enclosure in 1852
- Chapel Lane: long narrow fields adjacent to Chapel Lane (the droveway leading from the Common to Sayers Farm) derived from the Enclosure roadside waste in 1852.

Analogy with elsewhere suggests the origins of a number of other field boundary patterns:
- woodland assarting: the clusters of small rectilinear fields associated with the isolated farms at Solby's Farm, Scrub House, Bramble Hall, Garrold's Farm (and possibly Common Hall Farm)
- former open fields: the large–medium-sized rectilinear fields, with occasional reversed-S shaped boundaries, dog-legs in boundaries,[7] and long narrow fields laid out between slightly sinuous axial boundaries to the south (and possibly east) of the village are suggestive of open fields enclosed through agreement and resulting in the retention of strip and furlong boundaries. Further support for this interpretation comes from the Tithe Survey field-names that show two blocks of fields with the same name: Stock Field and Broom Field (Fig 15.5)
- enclosed hill pasture: the irregular-shaped fields south of Sayers and Castle Farms on the southern hills are not diagnostic of a particular process though their large

Figure 15.4: Hadleigh, Essex: selected landscape components: settlement, roads, commons, woodland, reclaimed marshland. Relict landscape features are shown with dashed lines: the Castle, fishponds, mill creek, and the extent of the former medieval deer park. Note that today the road south of Sayers Farm has also been abandoned but still survives as an earthwork (two parallel ditches with hedged banks): a relict feature that still makes a contribution to the historic landscape's character (drawing: the author)

size, and the steep-sided slopes that dominate this area, suggest a predominantly pastoral use
- the small enclosures immediately adjacent to the village and rectory are typical of the gardens, orchards etc found around agricultural settlements.

woodland (Fig 15.4)
A large block of woodland still survives to the north of the village, which was even more extensive in 1777.

unenclosed land (Fig 15.4)
The common was enclosed in 1852; unenclosed saltings still survive to the south of the sea wall.

military facilities
The ruins of the 13th-/14th-century Hadleigh Castle still dominate the Thames Estuary (Figs 10 and 15.4). During the Second World War, the strategic importance of Hadleigh's location was once again recognised when a searchlight and gun battery was built to the south of Sayers Farm to contribute to the protection of London.

water (Fig 15.4)
Earthworks of former fishponds survive on the marshes, while a dam in the valley north of the castle may also have been for a fishpond within the former deer park. Hadleigh Hall was formerly moated.

status, power, and tenurial structure
Hadleigh was a royal manor upon which a major transformation occurred with the construction of the castle and adjacent park in the 1230s, the latter impinging upon the village's field system (documentary material relating to this royal estate is summarised in Rippon 1999a). The estate was sold off in the 16th century, eventually leading to the enclosure of the park. Much of the former royal estate along with Sayers Farm to the west was purchased in 1890 by The Salvation Army who undertook a further transformation of the landscape in the late 19th/early 20th century through the creation of the Home Farm Colony with its extensive agricultural facilities (piggeries, dairies, orchards etc), brickworks, and an associated tramway system (Yearsley 1998, 51–65).

The northern part of the parish has a very different history. Large areas of woodland were held by several ecclesiastical institutions.[8] The conservative nature of these absentee landlords probably accounts for the relative stability in this part of the landscape. The remaining areas were part of a series of presumably freehold tenements documented from at least the 14th/15th centuries.[9] The extent of the landholding associated with these farms at the time of the Tithe Survey is shown on Figure 15.7).

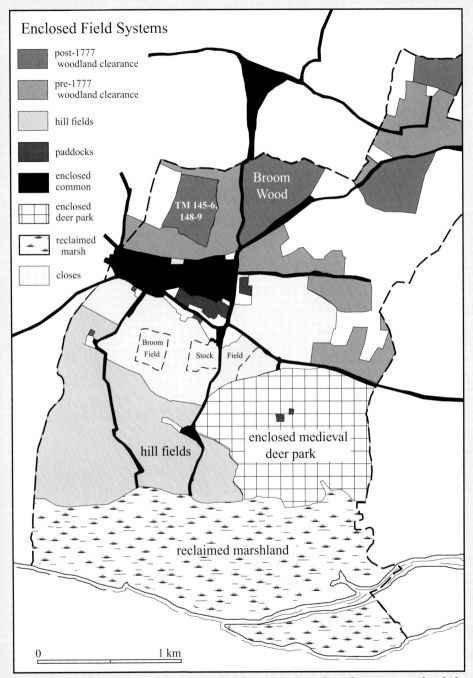

Figure 15.5: Hadleigh, Essex: enclosed field systems (based on the processes that led to their formation) (drawing: the author)

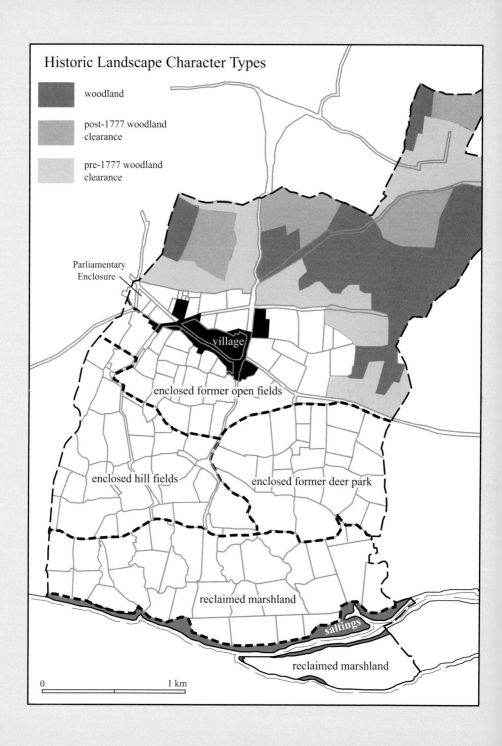

Historic Landscape Character Types

Legend:
- woodland
- post-1777 woodland clearance
- pre-1777 woodland clearance

Parliamentary Enclosure

village

enclosed former open fields

enclosed hill fields

enclosed former deer park

reclaimed marshland

saltings

reclaimed marshland

0   1 km

Historic landscape character types

Whilst it is convenient to disaggregate the landscape into its different component parts, in practice each of these cannot be understood in isolation from each other. The way that different components interact with each other helps to define a series of *generic* **historic landscape character types** (Fig 15.6):
- woodland
- pre-1777 woodland clearance
- post-1777 woodland clearance
- Parliamentary Enclosure
- village (nucleated settlement)
- dispersed settlement
- enclosed former open fields
- enclosed former deer park
- enclosed hill fields
- reclaimed marshland
- unenclosed saltings.

In many places these types have a clear boundary. In some cases these are long, straight or sinuous field boundaries that are easily identifiable in the field boundary pattern: the line of former park pale is still preserved as a field boundary, most of the surviving woodland is surrounded by a substantial earthen bank, while the edge of the reclaimed marshland is marked by the sea wall and a hedge bank running along the fen-edge. The southern edge of the enclosed former open field is also marked by a long sweeping boundary, though north of Sayers Farm its boundary with enclosed hill fields is less clear from the cartographic sources. In other landscape studies, fieldwork might resolve such issues though in the case of Sayers Farm, housing development and agricultural intensification (ie field boundary loss) have removed all evidence.

Historic landscape character areas

The mapping of these various *generic* historic landscape character types can then be simplified into the five *unique* **character areas** within Hadleigh (Fig 15.7):

character area	*character defining features*
1. Village	settlement: nucleated greenside village
	fields: small paddocks/orchards/gardens
	enclosed former open fields
	unenclosed land: former common and
	roadside waste along the droveways
	woodland: absent

Figure 15.6: Hadleigh, Essex: historic landscape character types (with a background of Hadleigh as depicted on the First Edition Six Inch survey of 1867). Three types related to the former extent of woodland are shaded as they occur in various places within the parish. The other types occur only once though they are found throughout the adjacent parishes (drawing: the author; reproduced from the 1867 Ordnance Survey map)

47

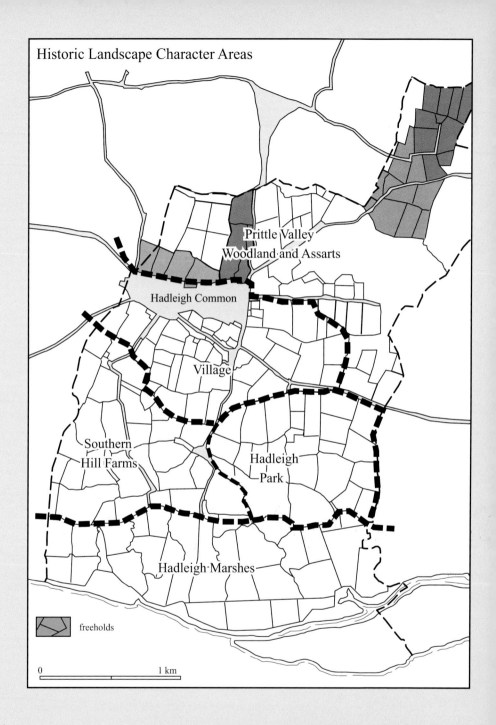

Historic Landscape Character Areas

Prittle Valley
Woodland and Assarts

Hadleigh Common

Village

Southern
Hill Farms

Hadleigh
Park

Hadleigh Marshes

freeholds

0   1 km

	lordship and community: moated manorial complex (Hadleigh Hall) beside the church; adjacent village with probable open fields to the south and east
2. Southern Hill Farms	settlement: isolated farms
	fields: large fields of irregular shape (largely pastoral)
	unenclosed land: roadside 'waste' along the droveways until 1852
	woodland: very occasional small copses
	lordship and community: partly former royal demesne farm (Castle Farm) and partly freehold (Sayers Farm) – the historic landscape character in these is not distinguishable; later part of Salvation Army Home Farm Colony
3. Hadleigh Park	settlement: single isolated farm (site of park lodge)
	fields: large rectilinear fields surrounded by line of former park pale
	unenclosed land: none
	woodland: absent
	lordship and community: former royal medieval deer park; later part of Salvation Army Home Farm Colony
4. Hadleigh Marshes	settlement: absent
	fields: reclaimed marshes
	unenclosed land: saltings to seaward of sea wall
	woodland: absent
	lordship and community: partly in former royal estate and partly freehold (Sayers Farm

---

Figure 15.7: Hadleigh, Essex: historic landscape character areas (with a background of Hadleigh as depicted on the Tithe Map of 1847) (drawing: the author).
1: village (nucleated village beside common, associated paddocks, and currently enclosed (but formerly open?) fields.
2.i: southern hills: isolated farms, irregular enclosed pastoral fields.
2.ii: southern hills: former deer park (note slightly greater regularity in field boundary pattern).
3: marshland (largely reclaimed but with fringe of open saltmarshes).
4: woodland and assarts (freehold farms).

and various monastic estates); later part of
Salvation Army Home Farm Colony

5. Prittle Valley Woodland and Assarts:
settlement: isolated farmsteads
fields: pre-1777 piecemeal woodland assarting
post-1777 woodland clearance
unenclosed land: roadside 'waste' along the
droveways until 1852
woodland: abundant
lordship and community: series of woods held by
remote ecclesiastical institutions, and
several freehold farms

Discussion

The historic landscape of Hadleigh can be disaggregated into a series of components
that come together to form a number of generic types that in turn can be grouped into
fewer, unique character areas. The morphology and spatial configuration of these
landscape components, alongside other sources of information such as early maps,
place-names and documentary references, allows the various processes that led to the
creation and subsequent evolution of this landscape to be unravelled. The medieval
landscape was focused around the common that occupies the central area of the
interfluvial plateau (such greenside settlement is typical of south-east England and
East Anglia: eg Williamson 2003, fig 30). Land to the south and east appears to have
been laid out in a small open field system, which may have been impinged upon by the
creation of the medieval deer park in the 13th century. The village community was
linked to outlying farms and other resources, such as woodland and marshland,
through a series of droveways. Subsequent changes to the landscape included the
reversion of the deer park to agricultural use probably in the 17th century, the
drainage of the marshes after 1670, the assarting of woodland both before and after
1777, and the enclosure of the open fields that must have been carried out by agreement without the need for an Act of Parliament. These changes clearly demonstrate
just how dynamic the historic landscape is at a certain level, but it should also be
remembered that certain key character defining features of the Hadleigh landscape
appear to have been more enduring: the basic four-fold division of marshland, the
southern hills (with large enclosed fields, occasional farmsteads, and little woodland),
the central plateau (the village and its associated field system), and the Prittle Valley
(with woodland, assarts, and isolated farmsteads) can be traced back well into the
medieval period.

The case study has also shown how we cannot understand historic landscape
character purely on the basis of morphology. The different character areas in Hadleigh
resulted from the different timescales and trajectories of change, in this case the
decisions of landlords and tenants to exploit different parts of the landscape in
different ways. In the central area the village *community* was dominant, with its
nucleated settlement, large common, and probable open fields. Beyond this there was
a landscape where the *individual* was dominant with a series of isolated farmsteads

associated with enclosed fields. The woodland survived due to the *conservatism* of several large ecclesiastical institutions located many miles away, while the south-east of the parish was dominated by a magnificent royal residence, and a landscape *transformed* through the creation of a deer park, its subsequent enclosure, and then the creation of Home Farm Colony by the Salvation Army. Hopefully, this case study has shown how adjacent places can have very different histories, and that historic landscape analysis can make a significant contribution to understanding how the environment has changed through human intervention, and how this history still affects the local landscape.

SUMMARY SO FAR

The British countryside displays marked regional variation in character reflecting its geology/topography/natural ecological potential and the varied cultural/historical factors affecting how it was exploited by human communities in the past and present. This regional variation was certainly recognised by early topographical writers and historic landscape analysis is a means of describing and understanding how it came about. The natural/physical background and the historic landscape that overlies it can be mapped in two dimensions (eg different patterns of settlement and field systems), but can only be understood when time-depth is added in order to grasp the different process of landscape creation and change. From the discussion so far, a number of key facets of the cultural landscape should have emerged:

Historic landscape analysis has developed from local/regional history, historical geography and landscape archaeology and is not a single technique, but an approach to describing/mapping spatial variation in landscape character, most notably as a means of **integrating** a wide range of archaeological and documentary material.

The **physical fabric** of the historic landscape:
- the rural countryside comprises a series of interrelated **elements/parcels** (eg individual fields, settlements, and roads) and **components** (eg field systems, settlement patterns, and communications networks), that together combine to create generic landscape **types/zones** of different character
- all these aspects of the cultural landscape must be studied together rather than in isolation: the way in which the individual components **articulate** with each other is fundamental to understanding historic landscape character
- in different areas the particular components, types, and zones combine in unique ways, leading to distinctive local character **areas**. At a regional scale these can be regarded as analogous to French *pays*, and at a national scale can be generalised as the 'champion' and 'woodland' landscapes (corresponding to Rackham's planned and ancient countryside, and Roberts and Wrathmell's Central, and South-Eastern and West and North-Western Provinces).
- **relict landscapes**, vernacular **architecture** and **building materials** (including field boundaries etc) also make a significant contribution to historic landscape character.

51

The **linguistic** dimension of the historic landscape – place-names and field-names – also make a significant contribution to regional variation in landscape character, as well as to our understanding of how the landscape has evolved and what it looked like in the past.

The cultural/social dimension (**human agency**): the landscape is the product of a wide range of cultural processes, interacting with the physical environment, and human agency has been instrumental in shaping biodiversity and habitats.
- the term 'natural beauty' is misleading in not acknowledging the cultural contribution to landscape
- although the natural character of the environment provides a broad framework which is relatively unaltered, there is a complex interaction of social, aesthetic and economic behaviour that has both been influenced by and has shaped physical cultural features draped over the basic geological/topographical framework
- different patterns of landownership, land tenure, and community clearly influenced historic landscape evolution and are often crucial to understanding differences in the physical fabric of the countryside.

The temporal dimension (**time-depth**) of the historic landscape:
- landscapes have a **time-depth** resulting from various historical processes, operating in different places and at different times, that led to marked regional variation in landscape character
- most landscapes will be a **palimpsest** of features from different periods, though some areas will have a character that is dominated by one or more major processes/events
- understanding this temporal dimension is essential in planning for the **future** if valued aspects of the landscape's character are to be maintained
- the historic landscape is a still-functioning part of the archaeological record (the **buried-relict-historic** landscape continuum) and as such should be studied alongside those buried and relict landscapes that were contemporary.

PART TWO
APPROACHES AND METHODS

Growing awareness of the historic landscape as a cultural and academic resource presents two problems: from the research perspective there is the sheer volume of potential information that is locked up within the physical fabric of the countryside, while from the management perspective there is the problem of how to deal with a cultural resource that is simply everywhere. It has been shown in Part One that landscapes are dynamic and ever-changing and will continue to evolve, but if they are to retain the essential characteristics that led to their being so highly valued in the first place, then this evolution must be managed. One cannot manage what one does not understand, and therefore historic landscape analysis is of value to planners and countryside managers in two ways: firstly, it identifies what the present landscape comprises (including the key character defining features), and secondly, it can then be used to inform decisions about how future change can be accommodated: what Bloemers (2002, 90) has described as 'future-oriented archaeology'. Analysis of the historic landscape is also an important element of 'past-oriented' research into the origins and development of our countryside, notably its ability to infer process from morphology and to provide a framework for the integration of a wide range of disparate sources.

The second part of this handbook looks at these issues in more depth by reviewing the development of different approaches towards historic landscape analysis by researchers and heritage managers in England, Scotland and Wales. Part Three describes selected examples in greater detail. The aim is to present the reader with a range of possible approaches to unlocking the wealth of information contained within the physical fabric of the countryside. These approaches can be tailored to particular projects and the handbook does not attempt to present a single 'standard' technique, though certain key points of good practice are identified in Part Four.

THE HISTORIC LANDSCAPE IN PLANNING FOR THE FUTURE: RECENT DEVELOPMENTS WITHIN BRITAIN

England: 'Historic Landscape Characterisation'

In 1991, a Government White Paper *This Common Inheritance* invited English Heritage to consider preparing a list of landscapes of historic importance to complement the *Register of Parks and Gardens of Special Historic Interest*, with the intention of identifying areas of landscape that were deemed to be of particular historical importance and therefore worthy of greater protection. This led English Heritage to instigate a research and development project, carried out by Cobham Resource Consultants and the Oxford Archaeological Unit, to assess appropriate methodologies for identifying 'historic landscapes' (published as *Yesterday's World, Tomorrow's Landscape*: Fairclough *et al* 1999), alongside a pilot project in Cornwall (see Part

Three), and the secondment of English Heritage's Graham Fairclough to the Countryside Commission to advise on the preparation of its policy statement *Views from the Past: Historic Landscape Character in the English Countryside* (Countryside Commission 1994a; 1996).

This early work led English Heritage to conclude that since the whole landscape has a historic dimension, the whole landscape is of value and as such should be subject to characterisation (see Fairclough 1994; 1995; 1999a, 1999b, 1999c; Fairclough *et al* 2002), and therefore a simple Register was not appropriate (*cf* Wales: see below). English Heritage's resulting approach has been to sponsor a series of **Historic Landscape Characterisation Projects** (HLCs) carried out by/on behalf of planning authorities (mostly counties, along with some 'Areas Outstanding Natural Beauty' and National Parks) (http://www.english-heritage.org.uk/Filestore/policy/pdf/countryside/boudless_horizons.pdf). This is in line with approaches to landscape assessment undertaken for non-historical reasons, the general purpose of which has been defined by the Countryside Agency (Countryside Commission 1993; Swanwick *et al* 1999) as assisting local authorities, landuse and conservation agencies and the private sector to:

- understand how and why landscapes are important
- promote the appreciation of landscape issues
- successfully accommodate new development within the landscape
- guide and direct landscape change.

The methodologies adopted in the earlier English Heritage sponsored HLCs have shown considerable variation, which was inevitable as both the philosophy behind HLC, and the technology available, was both new and evolving (Aldred and Fairclough 2003). The pilot project in Cornwall (see case study in Part Three), along with its immediate successors[10] can be considered as the first generation of HLCs. They were paper-based, or used newly available if primitive GIS, and entailed ascribing each parcel of landscape to one of a series of predetermined 'historic landscape types' which in turn were simplified into 'zones'. These early HLCs established a series of key principles:

- that the whole landscape is historic including semi-natural environments (such as unenclosed upland pasture)
- that the historic landscape is ever present, all around us and always changing
- that the basis for mapping is the modern landscape (though in contrast to later HLCs, extensive use was made of earlier cartographic sources in order to gauge the degree of recent change within the landscape)
- the sources used were systematic and region-wide
- the methodology was objective, transparent, and repeatable.

The next 'generation' of HLCs saw several methodological changes.[11] Most notable was the use of GIS (though by digitising paper-based work rather than using a fully electronic map-base) which allowed every single parcel of landscape to be assessed and/or tagged with a set of 'attributes' (size, shape etc) to which an interpretation could then be added to define blocks of uniform 'historic landscape character type' (eg Hampshire: Colour Plate B). These second generation HLCs took longer than the earlier examples, but dispensed with the use of earlier cartographic sources, lacked such detailed interpretative commentaries, and moved towards more morphological descriptions.

The third 'generation'[12] of HLCs in England started to see GIS reach its full potential in that the 'base-map' was itself electronic. The use of GIS also facilitates the integration of HLC with other sources (eg digitally rectified air photographs, early cartographic sources, and other databases such as Sites and Monuments Records). This allowed each 'polygon' to be tagged with increasing numbers of attributes, and while there was a tendency for strongly morphological descriptions these could be interpreted through further appropriate tags. Another key aspect of this 'generation' of HLCs was the distinguishing of present and past historic landscape character where the two differed significantly (a feature of the first generation).

Based on the sixteen completed studies (along with some input from four projects in progress and three at the planning stage), in 2002 English Heritage undertook the 'National HLC Method Review', leading to two reports: a review of the methodologies used to date (Aldred and Fairclough 2003; http://www.english-heritage.org.uk/Filestore/ conserving/characterisation/1-Cover.pdf), and a more standardised methodology for future work (Fairclough 2002; http://www.english-heritage.org.uk/Filestore/conserving/ characterisation/HLCPDtemplate1stEd25nov.pdf). These reports advocate greater standardisation in both methodology and terminology, including a uniform set of 'broad types' (a move back to the interpretative 'zones' of the older schemes). This more standardised approach is reflected in the fourth wave of county-based HLCs, which are also seeing the greater use of earlier cartographic sources (a feature of the first generation).[13]

A feature of the early work in Cornwall that has not usually been continued is that the full sequence of historic landscape character types, zones, and areas were initially identified, though the map of areas has been left in draft form and not published (for an extract see Herring 1998, 47–8). Subsequent English Heritage sponsored HLCs have not identified 'historic landscape character areas' because the Countryside Agency's 'Countryside Character Initiative' (http://www.countryside.gov.uk/cci) have already mapped 'landscape character areas'. Whether '*historic* landscape character areas' are deemed useful is for these 'future-oriented' projects to decide; from a 'past-oriented' research perspective they are essential and equate to the *pays* and regions that early topographic writers were so keenly aware of (see above and Lambrick and Bramhill 1999).

Scotland: 'Landuse Assessment'

Historic Scotland and The Royal Commission on the Ancient and Historic Monuments of Scotland have been collaborating since 1996 in their version of HLC – Historic Landuse Assessment (HLA) – which aims to 'map the landuse of Scotland from a historical perspective, showing its functional complexity, and date of origin' (eg Colour Plate C; Dyson Bruce *et al* 1999; Dixon and Hingley 2002; Macinnes 2002a, b; Stevenson and Dyson Bruce 2002). The methodology was inspired by that of Cornwall but adapted substantially for the Scottish context. The term 'historic landuse' is used instead of 'historic landscape' for two reasons: firstly, Scottish Natural Heritage were concerned that the title 'historic landscape character assessment' was too close to their own 'landscape character assessments', which at the time (1994/5) were fairly new and just starting to be used by planning authorities (Stevenson and Dyson Bruce

2002, 52). The second reason was that the Scottish approach was to focus upon the physical remains of the cultural landscape that are inherently related to landuse, as opposed to the wider issues of perception that are sometimes a factor in the work in Wales (see below: Lesley Macinnes, pers comm, February 2003).

In contrast to many of the earlier English HLCs, but in common with more recent developments there (eg Cornwall: Herring and Tapper 2002) and in Wales, the Scottish methodology also considers relict landscapes and the contribution that they make to the character of the present countryside. Two categories of landuse type are, therefore, defined:

- Historic Landuse Types: reflecting historic landuse types in current use, which may include types that are several hundred years old in origin
- Relict Landuse Types: reflecting historic landuse types that are no longer maintained for their original purpose, but which have left a visible trace in the landscape, and also relict archaeological landscapes that may be mapped (Dixon and Hingley 2002, 86).

Initially 47 'historic landuse types' (eg crofting township, 18th-/19th-century rectilinear fields) were identified alongside 48 relict types (eg pre-improvement agriculture and settlement, abandoned 18th-/19th-century rectilinear fields) that in places were also a current type as they form the key character-defining feature of today's countryside.

It was well known that medieval settlements and field systems in the Highlands and Hebrides were swept away in the 18th- and 19th- century agricultural improvements, and now only survive as relict remains (Dodgshon 1993a; 1993b; 1994) and in occasional depictions in contemporary paintings (Smout 1996). An important result of the Scottish HLA has been to reveal the extent to which the Scottish landscape was remodelled in the 18th and 19th centuries, with the result that in the areas studied so far, the predominant features that give the countryside its present character are only up to 300 years old (Piers Dixon, pers comm, February 2003). Shetland and parts of Orkney stand out in this respect as being different. At first sight, Orkney is dominated by regimented field systems, as may be seen on Shapinsay where the whole island has been laid out to a single grid of fields. On west Mainland, however, there are elements of the landscape that relate to the pattern of settlement that preceded the agricultural improvements. Within the rectilinear fields and modern farmsteads there are clusters of smallholdings or crofts that have continued to occupy the site of their pre-improvement townships, comprising a pattern of scattered steadings and fields that are irregular in plan and small in scale in comparison with the neighbouring improved farmland. This is unusual because crofting townships in the western highlands and islands were laid out to a single plan that owed little to what went before, and in lowland areas small tenants, if they got any recognition at all, generally received plots of marginal land. Grimeston is an example of this continuity of settlement (Colour Plate C2–3). At the time of the First Edition Ordnance Survey map, the unenclosed fields of Grimeston and the scatter of tenants steadings may be discerned in a sea of unimproved pasture, except for the fields of an improved farm to the south-east. Today this pattern is inherent in the crofters' steadings and the irregular small fields surrounded by the rectilinear pattern of improved farmland (I wish to thank Piers Dixon for providing this case study).

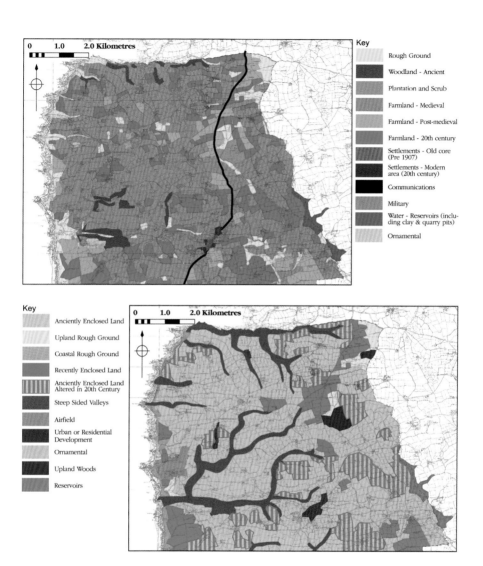

Key
0   1.0   2.0 Kilometres

- Rough Ground
- Woodland - Ancient
- Plantation and Scrub
- Farmland - Medieval
- Farmland - Post-medieval
- Farmland - 20th century
- Settlements - Old core (Pre 1907)
- Settlements - Modern area (20th century)
- Communications
- Military
- Water - Reservoirs (including clay & quarry pits)
- Ornamental

Key

- Anciently Enclosed Land
- Upland Rough Ground
- Coastal Rough Ground
- Recently Enclosed Land
- Anciently Enclosed Land Altered in 20th Century
- Steep Sided Valleys
- Airfield
- Urban or Residential Development
- Ornamental
- Upland Woods
- Reservoirs

0   1.0   2.0 Kilometres

Colour Plate A: The derivation of 'zones' from 'types' in the Cornwall HLC (© Cornwall County Council)

57

0   25 km

*Colour Plate B: Historic landscape types in Hampshire (a 'second generation'
English Heritage-sponsored HLC) (Fairclough* et al *2002, plate 8.1: © English
Heritage and Hampshire County Council). The map has had to be much reduced for
publication here but the detail can be found on the web (http://www.english-
heritage.org.uk/Filestore/conserving/characterisation/HampshireHLC.pdf). What
clearly emerges from Figure 15 is how some parts of the county have a relatively
simple and uniform character, while others are remarkably complex. Though broader
'character areas' are not identified in the final report, some are clearly emerging,
most obviously the well wooded New Forest (in the South West) and former
'champion landscape' on the chalk downland in the North West*

Hampshire Historic Landscape Types

1.1 Small irregular assarted fields
1.2 Medium irregular assarted fields
1.3 Large irregular assarted fields
1.4 Regular assarted fields
1.5 Former strips and furlongs
1.6 Regular fields - wavy boundaries
1.7 Irregular fields - straight boundaries
1.8 Regular 'ladder' fields
1.9 Small regular parliamentary fields
1.10 Medium regular parliamentary fields
1.11 Large regular parliamentary fields
1.12 Variable regular parliamentary fields
1.14 'Prarie' fields
1.15 Irregular fields bounded by roads
1.16 Small regular fields - wavy boundaries
2.1 Heathland commons
2.2 Downland commons
2.3 Other commons and greens
2.4 Wooded commons
3.1 Orchards
3.3 Nurseries with glasshouses
4.1 Assarted pre-1810 woodland
4.2 Replanted assarted pre- 1810 woodland
4.3 Other pre- 1810 woodland
4.4 Replanted other pre- 1810 woodland
4.5 C 19th plantations

4.6 Pre- 1810 hangers
4.7 19th- century hangers
4.8 Pre- 19th- century hangers
4.9 C 19th heathland plantations
4.10 Pre- 19th wood pasture
4.11 C 19th wood pasture
5.1 Unenclosed heath and scrub
5.2 Enclosed heath and scrub
5.3 Purlieus
6.1 Downland
7.1 Misc. valley floor enclosures
7.2 Valley floor woodlands
7.3 Marsh and rough grazing
7.4 Water meadows
7.5 Unimproved valley floor grass
7.6 Watercress beds
7.7 Fishponds, lakes and ponds
7.8 Watermill complexes
8.1 Coastal wetlands
8.2 Saltmarsh
8.3 Salterns
8.4 Reclaimed land
8.5 Harbours and marinas
8.6 Shingle and dunes
8.7 Mudflats
9.1 Scattered settlements in 1810
9.2 Scattered settlements post- 1810 extent

9.3 Common edge settlement 1810 extent
9.4 Common edge settlement post- 1810 extent
9.6 Post- 1810 settlement
9.7 Hamlet or village 1810 extent
9.9 Town and city 1810 extent
9.11 Caravan sites
10.1 Pre- 1810 parkland
10.2 Post-1810 parkland
10.3 Deer parks
11.1 Racecourses
11.2 Golfcourses
11.3 Major sports fields
12.1 Chalk quarries
12.2 Gravel pits
12.3 Factories
12.4 Large-scale industry
12.5 Water treatment reservoirs
12.6 Dockyards
13.1 Railway stations and sidings
13.3 Airfields
13.4 Motorway service areas
14.1 Prehistoric and Roman defence
14.2 Medieval defence
14.3 Post-medieval (1500-1830) defence
14.4 C19th (1830-1914) defence
14.5 C20th (1914-) defence

Colour Plate B (continued): key to historic landscape types in Hampshire

59

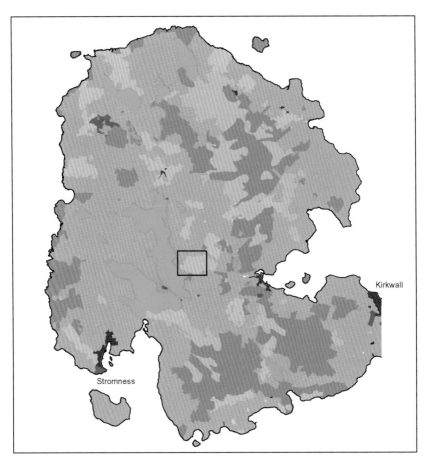

Colour Plate C1: Orkney Historic Landuse Assessment, with Grimeston inset (© Historic Scotland/RCAHMS)

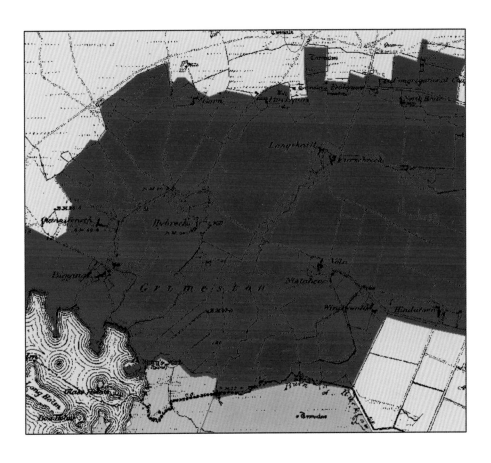

Legend

▦	Relict Early Prehistoric Ritual and Funerary Site
▨	18th-19th Century Planned Rectilinear Fields
▦	18th-19th Century Rectilinear Fields
■	18th-19th Century Smallholdings
▨	Rough Grazing
▢	Water

N

0   100   200   300   400 Meters

Colour Plate C2: Grimeston, with character types superimposed on the First Edition Six Inch map (© Historic Scotland/RCAHMS)

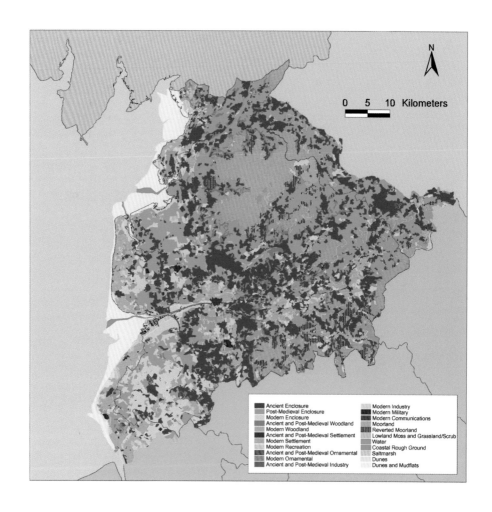

Legend entries:
Ancient Enclosure
Post-Medieval Enclosure
Modern Enclosure
Ancient and Post-Medieval Woodland
Modern Woodland
Ancient and Post-Medieval Settlement
Modern Settlement
Modern Recreation
Ancient and Post-Medieval Ornamental
Modern Ornamental
Ancient and Post-Medieval Industry
Modern Industry
Modern Military
Modern Communications
Moorland
Reverted Moorland
Lowland Moss and Grassland/Scrub
Water
Coastal Rough Ground
Saltmarsh
Dunes
Dunes and Mudflats

0 5 10 Kilometers

N

Colour Plate D1: Lancashire – general or entry level HLC types (© English Heritage and Lancashire County Council)

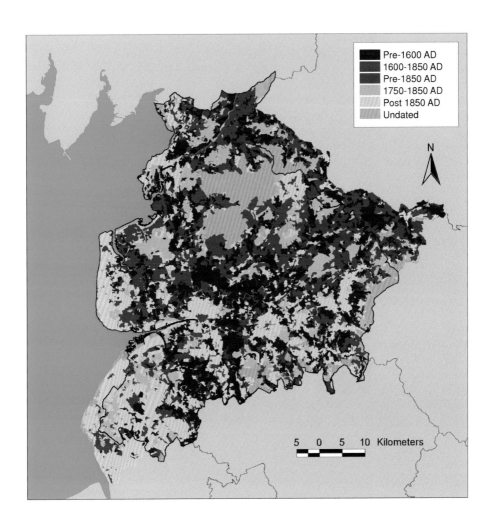

Legend:
- Pre-1600 AD
- 1600-1850 AD
- Pre-1850 AD
- 1750-1850 AD
- Post 1850 AD
- Undated

N

5 0 5 10 Kilometers

Colour Plate D2: Lancashire – phases of development (© English Heritage and Lancashire County Council)

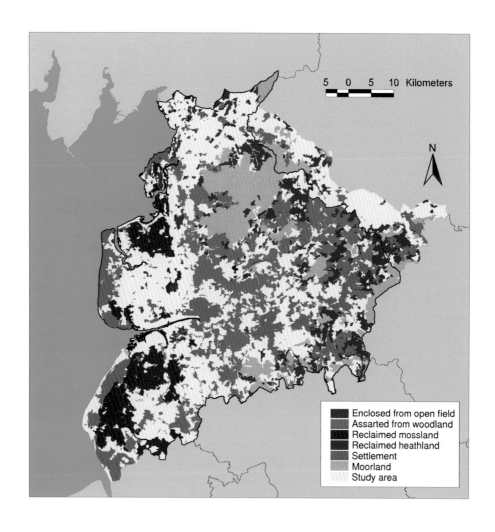

	Enclosed from open field
	Assarted from woodland
	Reclaimed mossland
	Reclaimed heathland
	Settlement
	Moorland
	Study area

Colour Plate D3: Lancashire – origins of enclosures (© English Heritage and Lancashire County Council)

Wales:

The Register of Landscapes of Historic Interest in Wales

In England and Scotland HLC/HLA is being used to establish the historic character of the landscape through a systematic 'bottom-up' analysis of entire regions, and a crucial characteristic of this approach is that no individual areas are identified as having particular importance. By contrast, in Wales, Cadw: Welsh Historic Monuments did follow the Government's suggestion in *This Common Inheritance* to develop a landscape register. In collaboration with the Countryside Council for Wales (CCW), the International Council on Monuments and Sites (ICOMOS), and working with the four Welsh Archaeological Trusts, the Royal Commission on the Ancient and Historical Monuments of Wales and the Welsh unitary authorities, it embarked upon the creation of the two-part *Register of Landscapes of Historic Interest in Wales* (Part Two of the *Register of Landscapes, Parks and Gardens of Special Historic Interest in Wales*: Cadw 1998; 2001). In an ideal world this would have been preceded by a 'bottom-up' HLC of the whole Welsh landscape to determine the range of historic landscapes present, the relative rarity/abundance of each type, their quality of preservation, and ultimately the relative importance of each type/area. However, as the experience in England and Scotland has since shown, this would have been a very long process and so the decision was taken that there was sufficient expertise amongst professional archaeologists, historians, and historical geographers working on the Welsh landscape to identify the most important areas through a 'top-down' approach. From over a hundred consultations, there was a clear consensus as to the 36 outstanding landscapes and a further 58 special historic landscapes, and this ensured the speedy production of the Register, so that it could start to input into planning decisions (Fig 16).

In addition to areas of still-functioning historic landscape, the Welsh Register includes examples where relict remains make a major contribution to present landscape character, for example the prehistoric monument complexes of the Preseli Hills in Pembrokeshire, and post-medieval lead mining landscape of Holywell Common and Halkyn Mountain in Clwyd. Certain historic landscapes in the Register also have important cultural associations such as the Vale of Dolgellau's early Quaker community, and the inspiration that the Lower Wye Valley provided for the Reverend William Gilpin's treatise on the notion and depiction of landscape as picturesque.

The Gwent Levels Historic Landscape Study

Alongside the creation of the *Register of Landscapes of Historic Interest in Wales*, Cadw and CCW also funded a detailed examination of one of the outstanding historic landscapes: the Gwent Levels. The Gwent Levels Historic Landscape Study was based upon in-depth research into the history and evolution of this *c* 111 sq km of reclaimed coastal marshland between Cardiff and Chepstow (Fig 16). It started with the desegregation of the historic landscape into its components/themes which were then reintegrated into a series of historic landscape types that were initially defined on the basis of morphology (variants of irregular, intermediate, and regular) and then the inferred process of their creation (eg piecemeal reclamation etc) – this is discussed further below: see Fig 17 and 20–1. The research was published as *The Gwent Levels: the evolution of a wetland landscape* (Rippon 1996a; and see Rippon 1995; 1997b) which essentially tells the story of how the landscape of today came into being, as far as it was understood at the time. Survey and excavation in advance of developments and coastal erosion have led to a series of subsequent archaeological investigations that have advanced our understanding of the prehistoric and Roman periods (Nayling and Caseldine 1997; Nayling 1998; Bell *et al* 2000; Rippon 2000c; Meddens 2001; and the journal *Archaeology in the Severn Estuary*), while work elsewhere has led to a more detailed mapping of the early phases of landscape development (see the case study on the Early Stages of Marshland Colonisation below).

A separate report *The Gwent Levels Historic Landscape Study: characterisation and assessment of the landscape* (Rippon 1996b; and see Rippon 1996a, fig 42) was designed to inform planners and countryside managers of the time-depth present in this remarkable landscape. This took the academic research into the origins and development of the landscape (the 'past-oriented' work) one step further in identifying a series of discrete and well-defined 'character areas', which were each described using the following criteria:

- **Location**: noting significant relationships to other character areas
- **Period**: including main period(s) of creation and modification
- **Components**: key character defining features such as field boundary and settlement patterns
- **Existing designations**: national and local planning and conservation designations
- **Condition**:
  - % of the Gwent Levels that this character area comprised *c* 1880 (base-mapping being the First Edition Six Inch maps)
  - % of the original (*c* 1880) area surviving
  - % field boundaries lost since *c* 1880
  - % of fields having seen agricultural improvement.
- **Documentation and association**
- **Current proposed developments**
- **Significance and value**: identification of the key features of this historic landscape character area.

The Gwent Levels are an example of a discrete physical *pays* that in part was occupied by communities whose territories (ie manors or parishes) were restricted to the marshland, although parts of the lower-lying backfens were exploited by communities living on the fen-edge and whose territories embraced both wetland and dryland. During the post-medieval period large amounts of land on the Levels was owned or leased by farmers living elsewhere and used as 'accommodation' land to fatten up livestock over the summer, and this seasonality is reflected in field-names such as 'Summerlease', and droveways such as 'Summerway'. If the Gwent Levels study had been a purely past-oriented research project into historic patterns of landuse then the

Figure 16: Areas of Wales included in the Register of Landscapes of Historic Interest in Wales *(Cadw 1998; 2001), with the Middle Wye Valley and the Gwent Levels highlighted. Inset: character areas within the Middle Wye Valley (source:www.cpat.org.uk/projects/longer/histland/midwye) (re-drawn by the author)*

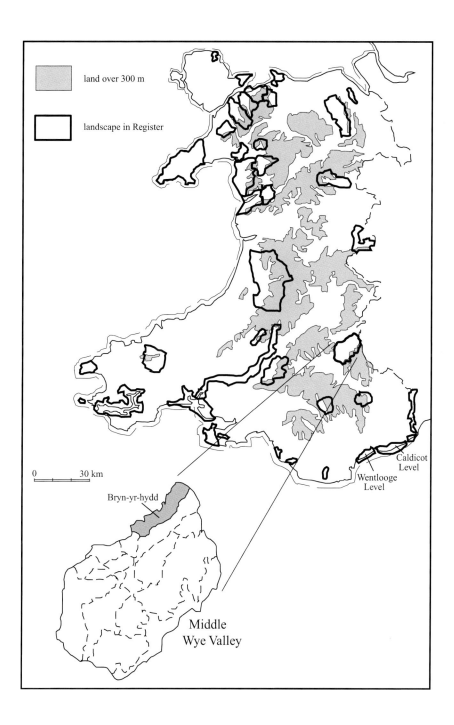

land over 300 m

landscape in Register

0   30 km

Caldicot Level

Wentlooge Level

Bryn-yr-hydd

Middle
Wye Valley

67

wetlands themselves would have to have been part of a far wider study area reflecting these wider socio-economic themes, as was published later (see Rippon 1997a).

Top-down historic landscape characterisation in Wales

Following the example of the Gwent Levels, the four Welsh Archaeological Trusts are currently carrying out detailed characterisations for each of the landscapes in the *Register*. For each landscape the report comprises a short introduction, followed by a description of nine '**historic landscape themes**' that cover the whole area:

* The natural landscape
* The administrative landscape
* Settlement landscapes
* Agricultural landscapes
* Transport and communications
* Industrial landscapes
* Defended landscapes
* Funerary, ecclesiastical and legendary landscapes
* Ornamental and picturesque landscapes.

These descriptions have a strong feel of historical narrative, introducing the user to how today's landscape character came into being. Following a 'top-down' approach each of the historic landscapes is then broken down into its discrete and unique historic landscape character areas as determined by the physical fabric of the countryside, landuse patterns, and a series of 'key historic landscape characteristics' that have shaped these areas:

* topography
* general settlement character
* description of settlements
* landuse today
* field patterns
* woodland
* roads
* mills
* quarries/industry
* churches/chapels
* parks and gardens
* sources.

This work can feed into the Countryside Council for Wales' landscape assessment methodology known as *LANDMAP*, and will inform various initiatives to protect and manage the Welsh countryside most notably the *Tir Gofal* agri-environmental scheme. An acronym for 'landscape assessment and decision-making process', *LANDMAP* has been developed by CCW in partnership with the Local and National Park Authorities, the Welsh Development Agency and other organisations with interests in landscape management. It aims to collect, collate, and evaluate information on landscape resources in Wales (geology, visual qualities, wildlife, as well as its cultural and historical interests) and to assess landscapes on a transparent and systematic basis. Assessors will examine a number of factors when describing a landscape and grading its worth. The methodology is GIS-based and has been devised to enable a wide range of information to be integrated into a single database capable of informing and supporting the needs of a variety of end-users and decision-makers concerned with landscape management. Once all-Wales cover is available, *LANDMAP* will become a powerful strategic tool to inform the sustainable use of landscape in Wales, including a historic landscape component.

CASE STUDY: THE CLWYD-POWYS ARCHAEOLOGICAL TRUST'S HISTORIC LANDSCAPE CHARACTERISATION OF THE MIDDLE WYE VALLEY (FIG 16)

Key features:

- *representative of the top-down identification of historic landscape character areas in Wales*
- *principal objective to inform planners and countryside managers*
- *a simple product making high level generalisations*
- *carried out by staff of the local archaeological unit, with a good local knowledge of the landscape and actively engaged in researching its archaeology/history*
- *further reading*: http://www.cpat.org.uk/projects/longer/histland/histland.htm Cadw, 1998 *Register of Landscapes of Outstanding Historic Interest in Wales*. Cardiff: Cadw Welsh Historic Monuments.

The following description, taken from the Historic Landscapes Register, *identifies the essential historic landscape themes in the historic character area as a whole.*

This distinctive Powys landscape lies to the south-west of Hay-on-Wye in the shadow of the Black Mountains, and runs from Hay Bluff at its north end to Mynydd Troed in the south. The landscape identified includes the floodplain and steeply sloped northern edge of the Wye valley, and the deeply incised plateau beneath the northern scarp of the Black Mountains.

This particular region of the Wye valley is in many ways similar to the Usk valley further to the south-west, around Brecon, typified by small, hedged fields enclosing the rich agricultural land on the valley floor between about 80 and 100 m above OD. To the south-east the land rises steeply onto the Black Mountains, which reach up to 700 m above OD, with evidence of agrarian encroachment along the lower slopes, rising onto the open moorland beyond. The area has a rich and varied history with important cultural associations.

Along the southern side of the valley, on the edges of the upland, lie a series of important Neolithic funerary monuments of a type known, because of their distinctive form and plan, as Severn-Cotswold tombs. These tombs were in recurrent use as communal repositories for the remains of the dead during the later half of the 4th millennium BC. There are impressive tombs surviving at Penywrlodd (Llanigon), Little Lodge, Pipton, Fostyll, and Penywrlodd (Talgarth). Among the other impressive prehistoric monuments in the area is the Pen-y-Beacon Bronze Age stone circle on the edge of the Black Mountains.

Although much of the area owes its appearance to Anglo-Norman influences, there is significant evidence for native Welsh settlement. Glasbury is thought to have originally been a *clas* foundation (the administrative centre of a monastic unit of settlement in medieval times), and it is also recorded as being the site of the Battle of Clasbirig in 1056 between the Saxons and the Welsh. Llyswen is reputedly focused on another *clas* church, founded during the 6th century, and there is documentary evidence for a religious site being given to the See of Llandaff in about AD 650.

The Anglo-Norman settlement is most clearly seen at Hay-on-Wye, which still retains its medieval street plan, with remnants of the castle and town defences. Today, the town is best known for its bookshops and the annual festival of literature. Across the Wye from Hay lies the site of the Roman fort alongside the river, and beyond it, Clyro, made famous by the diary of the Reverend Francis Kilvert, who lived in the village in the 1870s. Although many of the places described by Kilvert are currently outside the area described here, the lifelike account he has left of the places and people he knew, has caused the region centred upon Clyro to become known as Kilvert Country, and to become a place of literary pilgrimage. Other important medieval settlements include Talgarth and Bronllys, both of which had extensive open arable field systems surviving up to the middle of the 19th century, that of Bronllys having been only enclosed in 1863. Many of the small villages are thought to have had early medieval origins and some, such as Llanfilo, display important earthwork remains relating to their former medieval extents.

Trefecca is famous for Trevecca College founded in the mid-18th century by Howell Harris, who was well-known for founding early Welsh Methodist societies, assembling a community of about 100 followers at his home, Trevecka Fach, in 1752. The community was influential in printing religious books and also for agricultural improvements.

Along the northern slopes of the Black Mountains lie several commons, such as Tregoyd Common and Common Bychan, which preserve their post-medieval field systems. The landscape here contrasts strongly with the moors to the south-east and the hedged landscape of the valley floor.

*There follows discussion of each of the **historic landscape themes** listed above, and the Middle Wye valley is then broken down into a series of **historic landscape character areas**, each with a detailed description. The following example illustrates the systematic discussion of the archaeological/historical background, the present landscape appearance including the standing buildings, relict remains that still contribute to the present character of the landscape, and cultural associations.*

Bryn-yr-hyddand Glasbury, Powys (Historic Landscape Character Area 1082)

Summary
Small medieval nucleated church and castle settlements on valley edge, and medieval and later scattered farmsteads on lower-lying hill land in landscape of small irregular fields, representing gradual encroachment on upland commons.

Historic background
Early settlement in the area is indicated by scatters of flintwork of Mesolithic, Neolithic and early Bronze Age date, a Neolithic polished stone axe, and the remains of the Neolithic chambered tomb at Court Farm, just to the south-west of Clyro. Settlement in the Iron Age period is suggested by the earthwork

enclosure on Bryn-yr-hydd Common. The character area fell along the southern edge of the Welsh medieval kingdom of *Elfael*, whose boundary at this point lay along the river Wye on the south and probably along the line of Cilcenni Dingle on the west. The area formed part of the medieval ecclesiastical parishes of Clyro and Llowes. The earliest evidence relating to St Meilig's church, Llowes, is a decorated cross of the 11th century, but both the church and the settlement around it possibly date to the early medieval pre-Conquest period. The early history of St Michael's Church at Clyro is less clear. Parts of the church are possibly of early 15th-century date, though the church and associated settlement may have been first established in association with the earthwork and stone castle, known as La Royl, to the south-east of the village. The castle is first mentioned in 1396, but it may have had its origins in the period between the late 11th to 13th centuries. Castle Kinsey motte and bailey at Court Evan Gwynne is again likely to belong to this period. Buildings at Court Farm, Clyro, include part of medieval stone buildings probably belonging to a monastic grange of Cwmhir Abbey, Radnorshire. At the Act of Union in 1536 the area fell within the hundred of Painscastle in Radnorshire. In the mid-19th century the area fell within the tithe parishes of Clyro and Llowes.

Key historic landscape characteristics

The area occupies low, south-facing undulating hills, overlooking the floodplain of the river Wye, between a height of between 80 and 244 m above OD. The soils are predominantly well drained fine reddish loams overlying sandstone bedrock (Milford Series). The present-day landuse is predominantly pasture, with areas of modern conifer plantation on steeper slopes, as at Cwm-Sirhwy Wood, Forest Wood and Pen-y-lan. There are some areas of ancient semi-natural broadleaved woodland along some of the steep-sided stream valleys such as Clyro Brook, Garth Dingle, Fron Wood and Cilcenni Dingle. Small remnant areas of unenclosed upland common land survive at Llowes Common and Bryn-yr-hydd Common, with birch scrub and bracken.

The present-day settlement pattern includes the small nucleated villages at Clyro and Llowes on low-lying ground on the edge of the floodplain of the Wye, together with a pattern of dispersed medium-to-small-sized farms about 300–900 m apart, mostly on the higher ground, in many cases lying within their own lands and approached by farm tracks. The large country house of the 1840s at Clyro Court is approached by a long drive to the south-west of Clyro and is set out in a dominating position above the former turnpike road to the south.

Surviving medieval buildings include part of the fabric of St Michael's Church at Clyro and the pointed arches in a barn at Court Farm, Clyro, which are believed to be part of a monastic grange belonging to the Cistercian abbey at Cwmhir.

A number of building platforms on sloping ground to the north of the village of Llowes possibly represent abandoned medieval or later house sites. The earliest surviving domestic buildings are of late medieval to early post-medieval date and include a number of cruck-framed timber buildings rebuilt in stone in the 17th–19th centuries. This building horizon is represented by several dwellings in the village of Clyro, the Old Vicarage and Radnor Arms in

Llowes (both of which are based on late medieval hall houses), and Bryn-yr-hydd farmhouse and barn, the farmhouse at Bryn-yr-hydd possibly being derived from a longhouse plan. Other farmhouses, and larger and smaller dwellings built anew in the 17th to early 19th centuries are generally of stone rubble, as at Moity farmhouse, Parciau, and cottages within the villages of Clyro and Llowes. A number of 17th- to 18th-century stone farm buildings survive, occasionally with stone gable walls and weatherboarded sides, including a linear range of buildings at Moity Farm, Gaer Farm, a hay barn at Court Evan Gwynne and a converted stone hay barn within the village of Llowes. Stone rubble, sometimes rendered or roughcast, continued to be the predominant building material in the area in the 18th and early to mid-19th century, as in the case of houses and farmworkers' cottages within the village of Llowes and Clyro, including some with brick window and door dressings. Local stone roofing tiles were probably commonplace before the widespread adoption of slate in the later 19th century. Stone tiles survive on a number of buildings, including the Old Vicarage, the Radnor Arms and Barn Cottage in Llowes, and Sacred Cottage and a number of other cottages in Clyro.

Clyro in particular expanded following improvements to the road system from the later 18th century onwards. Notable buildings of this period including the earlier 19th-century Baskerville Arms Hotel, Clyro Court (now the Baskerville Hall Hotel), the former stables and coachhouse to Clyro Court (now Cil y Beiddiau), and the stone-built Victorian school and Schoolmaster's House. Clyro Court and a number of later 19th-century buildings, such as the Vicarage House at Llowes, were built in ashlar masonry, or had ashlar dressings.

Traces of ridge and furrow on the west side of Clyro possibly represent former medieval open fields belonging to the village. The modern agricultural landscape is dominated by small and irregularly shaped fields, with lynchet formation on the steeper slopes indicating more widespread cultivation in the past. Most of the field boundaries are formed of multi-species hedges, including hazel, holly, and blackthorn. Small areas of unenclosed land at Bryn-yr-hydd Common and Llowes Common appear to represent the remnants of more extensive areas of upland grazing, perhaps enclosed during the course of the 18th century. Relatively late enclosure appears to be indicated by a pattern of medium-sized rectangular fields with single-species hedges to the north-west Llowes Common, in the area between Old Forest and Fforest-cwm. A number of the upland farms evidently represent earlier phases of encroachment in the medieval and late medieval periods, with occasional drystone wall field boundaries and low clearance banks on some of the higher ground. Many of the farms and houses in the area were associated with orchards in the 19th century, particularly in the area around Clyro, of which some remnants survive.

A pattern of early winding roads, lanes, and footpaths links the farms, townships, and village centres, many of which are likely to be of medieval origin. The lanes generally skirt around the field boundaries, some occupying hollow-ways up to 3 m or more in depth, which formed in the period before the introduction of metalled road surfaces. Surviving from the turnpike era of road transport are milestones near Clyro, Courtway, and Llowes and Bronydd.

Processing industry is represented by several former water-powered cornmills. Llowes Mill on Garth Brook, a tributary of the Wye is first mentioned in the 1840s; it ceased working in about 1920 and is now derelict. The Clyro Brook in the village of Clyro once provided power for two water-powered cornmills, Pentwyn Mill and Paradise Mill, both possibly of 18th-century origin. Pentwyn Mill had probably ceased working by 1840, whereas Paradise Mill was last worked in 1940. Extractive industry is represented by a number of small stone quarries which were probably worked for building stone from about the 17th century onwards.

Defensive structures within the area include the possibly Iron Age earthwork Bryn-yr-hydd enclosure, Castle Kinsey motte and bailey at Court Evan Gwynne, and Clyro Castle, which has a motte-like platform with possible foundations of a stone shell keep.

Important religious buildings include the churches within the medieval nucleated settlements at Llowes and Clyro, both of which were substantially rebuilt in the 1850s. The former early 19th-century New Zion Chapel near Moity Farm, is built of stone rubble. Like many nonconformist places of worship in the area it is characteristically sited in isolation on the higher ground, where it would have served a dispersed rural community.

In terms of cultural associations, the area is well known for its links with the writings of the diarist Francis Kilvert, curate of Clyro between 1864–76. Clyro Court is associated with Sir Arthur Conan Doyle who is said to have stayed at the house (built by the Baskerville family) to write *The Hound of the Baskervilles*, serialized in the *Strand Magazine* between 1901–02.

Source: http://www.cpat.org.uk/projects/longer/histland/histland.htm

Attributing value to historic landscape character

The use of HLC in Wales is very different to that in England and Scotland in terms of its top-down methodology, and the decision to identify certain areas of the historic landscape as being more important than others. English Heritage rejects this selective approach:

> There was ... a need for a comprehensive broad-based approach to landscape to counter the strong and well-intentioned (but ultimately misguided) desire in some quarters (some of whom ought to have known better) to 'solve' the problem of landscape protection by the selection of the 'best bits'. This would have taken us down more than one cul-de-sac, and we needed to avoid this by putting forward a more sensible, integrated approach (what is now called 'joined-up' thinking) (Fairclough 1999b, 5).

This is a contentious issue and HLC practitioners, planners, and countryside and heritage managers have some stark differences of opinion as to whether or not certain areas should be identified as being of greater historic value than others. While a detailed discussion is beyond the scope of this handbook, the issue should at least be aired so that the reader can start to form his/her own opinion (and see Foard and Rippon 1998).

The British planning system presently has as one of its underlying principles that we control development in areas of particular importance for their nature conservation value (eg Sites of Special Scientific Interest), visual character (eg Areas of Outstanding Natural Beauty and National Parks), architectural interest (eg Listed Buildings and Conservation Areas), and archaeological significance (Scheduled Ancient Monuments). The Welsh *Register* follows this approach for the historic landscape, while in contrast the English Heritage philosophy rejects the idea that some areas of the historic landscape (the 'best bits') are more important than others. Is it not the case, however, that some areas of historic landscape are better preserved than others, or have greater cultural associations? Has the debate between the English and Welsh approaches got too polarised ('to designate or not to designate'), and what we should be moving towards is a recognition that, whilst acknowledging that all landscapes have a historic dimension and all landscapes must continue to evolve, certain places have a greater capacity to absorb change of a certain nature than others? Where, for example, is it more appropriate to accom-modate a new industrial estate: on an area of well-preserved agricultural landscape which retains a wide range of historic features and has excellent documentary sources for the medieval period, or an area subject to intensive agricultural 'improvement' that has removed most of the historic landscape components? What might be the more appropriate course for a new motorway: through the middle of a well-preserved and unique 12th-century planned village and its associated field system, or on agricultural land of a fairly common type where there has already been significant field boundary loss, and adjacent to the existing urban/industrial fringe (so that the motorway simply represents a relatively limited extension of this urban/industrial zone)? In each of these cases, having assessed the historic landscape character of *all* these areas, and accepting that *each* has a value, it is surely quite clear that the proposed developments are more appropriate in the latter locations.

It is only possible for HLC to steer development away from the most sensitive areas in this way if specific *character areas* are identified, as value cannot be attributed to generic types or zones. Assessing the value of all areas is also not the same as desig-nating certain places and ignoring the rest. It advocates an objective description of historic landscape character across the *whole* region (county etc), and an assessment of each character area's importance in terms of its rarity, condition, cultural associa-tions etc. The comparison of modern and historic maps, for example, can allow certain areas of landscape to be identified that have experienced considerable change, and which will therefore be more able to accommodate future change than areas of historic landscape that are better preserved.

Some degree of change can be seen as not only acceptable but even beneficial, if it is compatible with the prevailing historic landscape character; the planting of small areas of mixed deciduous woodland on steeper hillsides within areas of 'ancient [ie medieval] enclosure' would be perfectly acceptable, as such valley-side woodland has always been an important part of the historic landscape character of such areas. Planting the same woodland on areas of a reclaimed coastal wetland would be totally unacceptable as there has never been such a habitat on these areas; small areas of alder woodland in the lowest-lying backfens of such wetlands would, in contrast, be an interesting development for although very little remains today, such a landscape component is historically well attested. The role of HLC here would be to advise a countryside manager proposing to plant woodland, of the location and species that are most in keeping with the historic landscape character.

There will probably never be agreement on whether the *designation* of particular historic landscapes as being of particular significance is a good or a bad thing: the approach certainly has its advantages and its disadvantages. What seems clearer is that a *comprehensive* HLC, uniformly carried out across a whole region (county, National Park etc) is of great benefit to planners and countryside managers who have the task of managing change throughout the historic landscape. Some 'change', however, amounts to wholesale destruction, and the extent to which universal characterisation should be used to identify certain types/areas as being of *particular significance*, so that such development avoids these places, or that characterisation will be used to identify other types/areas where change is more acceptable, will no doubt continue to be debated.

HISTORIC LANDSCAPE ANALYSIS AND UNDERSTANDING THE PROCESSES OF LANDSCAPE CHANGE

The discussion above has focused on how analysis of the historic landscape can be used to inform the planning process and countryside management. As such, this work has as its focus the mapping of today's landscape character, although both the early work in Cornwall and more recent HLCs incorporate historical map sources so that the degree of recent landscape change can be gauged. While 'forward-looking' in terms of their primary role, the careful design of these databases give them great potential for further research into the origins and development of our countryside and townscapes (eg see Cornwall case study in Part Three). There is far more to historic landscape analysis, however, than the principle that different landscape morphologies (settlement patterns, field boundary patterns etc) reflect different processes of landscape creation and evolution. As a form of historical research it becomes particularly effective when integrated with a wide range of other archaeological, documentary, and place-name evidence, and this is explored further in the rest of this section.

The integration of sources

A key feature of historic landscape analysis is that its physical fabric provides a framework for the mapping and integration of a wide range of sources:

* early cartographic sources that record the landscape at different stages in its development
* archaeological evidence, in terms of both 'relict' features and buried sites/landscapes, that forms parts of the historic landscape that have been abandoned, or relates to earlier, long since abandoned landscapes but which still contribute to historic landscape character
* documentary sources referring to components of the landscape, patterns of landuse, and landholding.

Documentary sources in particular contain a huge reservoir of information on past landscapes in terms of who held land and how it was used, and Britain has a long tradition of social, economic, and agrarian histories, notably of the great monastic estates whose archives have survived well (eg Finberg 1951; Keil 1964). All to often, however, the discussion of settlements, field systems, agriculture, and landholding takes a very 'abstract' form with little or no attempt to reconstruct what these landscape actually looked like. Historic landscape analysis can, however, achieve this as many Tithe Surveys and other early cartographic sources record place- and field-names which can be compared to those in earlier documents (see Field 1972; 1993; Richardson 2002). In Shapwick (Somerset), for example, post-Enclosure field-names preserve many medieval furlong names listed in a 16th-century survey which have enabled the structure of the open field system to be reconstructed (Aston *et al* 1998), while in nearby Meare 19th-century field-names can be traced back through a variety of 13th- to 16th-century sources allowing the sequence in which different areas were reclaimed to be established (see case study in Part Three).

The scale of research

The historic landscape can be studied at a wide variety of scales, and the size of a study area will be determined by a wide range of variables including:

- **aims of the project:** ranging from an in-depth investigation of a particular community and its landscape, through to the more rapid assessment of a limited number of facets of landscape character over a county or larger scale
- **resources:** the time and expertise available
- **sources:** the extent to which fieldwork, field- and place-names, historic maps and other surviving documentary sources are being used.

Examples of convenient study areas include:

- **parish/manor**: clearly defined territories that correspond to the communities and manors that were the basis of how the landscape was exploited on a day-to-day basis, and which led to the creation of many key landscape-related documentary sources (such as estate surveys, court rolls etc). Examples in this handbook: Hadleigh (see Part One); Meare (see Part Three).
- **district**: areas defined on the basis of physical topography and/or early territorial divisions. Example in this handbook: the Caldicot Level (Figs 17 and 20–21), a discrete and closely defined physical *pays* encompassed by four wholly marshland parishes and parts of ten others which extended onto the adjacent drylands. Another example of landscape study on this scale includes the eleven parishes of the Whittlewood Project (in Buckinghamshire and Northamptonshire), focused on a royal forest and the communities living around its fringes (Page and Jones 2000; Jones and Page 2001). The large early medieval estates that fragmented into the units that became the basis of medieval parishes would also make for convenient units of study (eg the eight Rodings parishes in Essex: Bassett 1997).

- **region**: larger-scale *pays* defined on the basis of broad physical divisions within the landscape giving rise to similar approaches by human communities towards their exploitation. Example in this handbook: Greater Exmoor (Fig 18), the 39 parishes spread across Devon and Somerset that extend down from the high moors and across the upland fringe.
- **county**: administrative unit that often bears little relationship to the cultural or physical landscape, though currently the basis for strategic planning. Convenient for research as many sources are organised on a county basis (eg Records Offices, Sites and Monument Records, County Records Society series, the Victoria County Histories, English Place-Name Society volumes). Examples in this handbook: Hampshire (Colour Plate B), Lancashire (Colour Plate D), and Somerset (Fig 27.1).
- **national**: in Scotland the plan is to apply HLA to the whole country, though in England methodological differences in the individual county-based HLC may make this difficult unless a 'top-down' approach is used. Roberts and Wrathmell (2000a; 2002) have completed a national characterisation of 19th-century settlement patterns that has enormous potential for correlation with other datasets (eg Darby's (1977) Domesday geographies, and Campbell (2000) and Thirsk's (1967b) farming regions (see Somerset case study in Part Three).

Historic landscape analysis could also be applied to a study area comprising scattered or disparate units. This might entail the comparison of a specific type of generic physical *pays* that occurs in various locations in order to compare how the same environment was exploited under different socio-economic conditions (eg under different patterns of landownership, and different proximities to centres of consumption) (eg coastal wetlands: Rippon 2000a). Another type of study could be an extensive but scattered estate such as those of the church (eg for ecclesiastical landholding in Somerset see Fig 27.14) or secular lordships (eg the Honor of Dudley: Hunn 1997).

Base maps in past-oriented historic landscape analysis

The 'future-oriented' HLCs now use GIS systems that have as their base modern 1:25,000 Ordnance Survey maps. In contrast, 'past-oriented' research should use the earliest appropriate cartographic sources that show the landscape at a level of individual fields before the degradations of 20th-century intensive farming. For historic landscape analysis covering large areas, the best source is the First Edition Ordnance Survey Six Inch Series (approximating to the modern 1:10,000 scale mapping), mostly surveyed between the 1860s and the 1880s (Oliver 1993, 30–4), and which should be available through most Records Offices or Local Studies Libraries. These maps are increasingly being used in digital form in HLCs. The First Edition Six Inch Series generally show the British landscape in a state of maturity, after the completion of what in many areas was a period of dramatic change in the 18th and 19th centuries, notably through the enclosure of open fields and common pasture, and the reorganisation of large parts of the Scottish landscape as part of the agricultural improvements. The First Edition Six Inch Series also predate the large-scale destruction of field boundaries that formed part of the later 20th-century agricultural intensification, and urban/industrial sprawl that has completely destroyed large areas of countryside. If the later 19th century represents a period of 'maturity' for the British landscape, the damage of recent decades to its historic coherence – such as the removal of field-boundaries, the drainage of wetlands, and cutting of peat – might represent its 'senility', and our insanity for allowing such destruction to happen, simply to produce mountains of unwanted food!

For smaller-scale study areas the Tithe Maps of *c* 1840 provide the earliest comprehensive mapping for most areas outside the Midland zone, where Parliamentary Enclosure had usually already extinguished tithe payments making a survey unnecessary (Kain and Prince 1985; Kain and Oliver 1995). For areas that were subject to Parliamentary Enclosure the resulting maps usually cover all or most of the parish after enclosure (Kain *et al* forthcoming), and earlier arrangement of the open fields normally requires the use of field evidence such as earthworks and documentary sources (eg Hall 1981). For a lucky handful of places there are earlier maps covering the entire parish (eg Meare: Fig 28.1), while most places have at least a few pre-1840 estate maps that cover smaller areas (eg Hadleigh: Fig 15.3).

Map regression/retrogressive analysis

For anyone used to interpreting the morphology of field systems and settlement patterns, the earliest cartographic source with comprehensive coverage of the study area provides the best starting point for historic landscape analysis (see above). In order to interpret a two-dimensional map of a historic landscape, however, one has to understand the processes behind its creation. For those new to landscape research there is a benefit in starting with far more recent cartographic sources, and seeing how the countryside changed over the last couple of centuries through studying a sequence of maps of the same area at different points in time (Williamson 1987 remains the seminal demonstration of this; and see Aston 1988c, fig 4.3; Hunn 1994). The best place to start is a modern map, and then the sequence of previous Ordnance Survey maps of the same area, and finally the Tithe Map along with any earlier estate maps (eg Figs 15.2–3). Such an approach is known as **map regression** or **retrogressive analysis** and is a key to understanding the processes of landscape change.

An obvious question to ask is why is it necessary to look through a sequence of recent maps when earlier ones exist: why not simply consult the earliest source? The answer is that retrogressive analysis is not simply about establishing what the landscape looked like in the past, but understanding the *processes* whereby landscapes change. Figure 17 shows the Caldicot Level, in south-east Wales, at two periods: in 1831 when it was mapped for the Commissioners of Sewers (who were responsible for maintaining the drainage system in this reclaimed wetland: Gwent Records Office D.1365/2) and 1880/1 when it was mapped by the Ordnance Survey for the First Edition Six Inch Series (published in 1886/7). A comparison of these maps shows several examples of the processes of landscape change. A number of areas were subject to Parliamentary Enclosure: a series of common 'wastes' associated with droveways in Redwick and Whitson (and see Fig 1), the common pasture of Caldicot Moor, and the open fields of Redwick. In the case of the last two, morphologically distinctive landscapes were created following enclosure, characterised by large rectangular fields, and long, straight, narrow roads, and once a number of such comparative exercises have been completed the landscape researcher will soon be able to recognise the

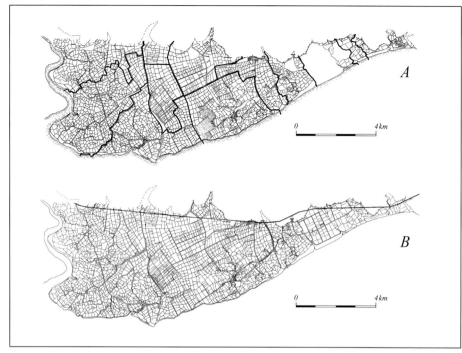

Figure 17: Caldicot Level 1831 (Commissioners of Sewers Maps: Gwent Records Office D.1365/2) and c 1880 (First Edition Ordnance Survey Six Inch maps) (redrawn by the author)

distinctive product of Parliamentary Enclosure. The enclosure of Whitson Common (and the other droveways) also resulted in a distinctive set of landscape features: the post-enclosure road was laid out down the centre of the common with long, narrow fields to either side representing the former roadside 'waste' (Figs 1 and 15.2). Another distinctive feature of the enclosure of this common is how the row of farmsteads that were next to the edge of the common are now set back from the post-enclosure road (and see Fig 12: Longham). The network of roads, droveways, and commons can be thought of as the skeleton of the historic landscape and their recon-struction in this way is often a good starting point when disaggregating a landscape into its component parts.

A comparison of the Caldicot Level in 1831 and 1880/1 illustrates another example of the process of landscape evolution, in this case how stratigraphic relationships can be used to establish the relative chronology of two landscape elements. The Great Western Railway from London Paddington to Cardiff sliced through the northern part of this landscape during the mid-19th century, and stratigraphically it clearly post-dates the earlier field and road system, creating small, awkwardly shaped, and sometimes even triangular parcels of land (and see Fig 15.2). Interestingly, there is a very similar set of oddly-shaped fields on the northern side of the sea wall which runs along the southern edge of the Level, and analogy with the railway line's relationship to its neighbouring field boundaries suggests that the sea wall similarly postdates the adjacent historic landscape. Other research has demonstrated that this was indeed the case, and that the sea wall was set back to its present location sometime in the late medieval period as a result of coastal erosion (Allen 1988; 2002; Rippon 1996a, 97–9).

Patterns of landholding in the historic landscape

Since the historic landscape was crafted by human hand, it is to be expected that different patterns of landholding/landownership will have had a far-reaching impact on the form that the landscape took. In the Hadleigh case study (see Part One) the communal regulation of the central area (the village, common and open fields) was contrasted with the dramatic impact of lordship on the royal estate, the small-scale and piecemeal asserting of the freeholders, and conservatism of the absentee ecclesiastical landowners (who held most of the woodland).

Another example of how an appreciation of the nature of landholding can assist in understanding the origins and development of the historic landscape is shown in Figures 18–19. Gillard's (2002) characterisation of the historic landscape in the Greater Exmoor region led to the identification of a distinctive landscape with small blocks of long, narrow, 'strip-like' fields associated with isolated farmsteads or small hamlets. The distribution of these 'type VIII' landscape features shows a marked bias towards the higher upland fringes, close to the upper limit of medieval/early post-medieval enclosure, some distance from what are assumed to have been the older settled lands around the parish churches. This location suggests that these were the colonising settlements of communities being forced to occupy some of the higher, more environmentally 'marginal' lands, while the field boundary morphology is suggestive of small formerly subdivided or common fields surrounded by larger closes probably held in severalty. This hypothesis was tested in a number of ways. Field survey showed that a number of the major linear boundaries that divided the blocks of different field morphology were more substantial than average, while an analysis of the Tithe Survey field-names identified several blocks of fields with both a common morphology and the same field-name (eg Newer Parks, Gratton and Holland: Fig 19A). The Tithe Survey also showed that the pattern of landownership in the blocks of small strip-like fields was extremely fragmented, in contrast to the larger closes that occurred in blocks of common ownership, supporting the hypothesis of a common-field core (now enclosed) with blocks of closes held in severalty beyond (Fig 19B). Such contrasting patterns of landownership have been noted elsewhere in the South West and alongside the physical fabric of the countryside, and patterns of field-names, can be a useful indicator of the structure and management of field systems (Aston 1988d, fig 5.6; Pattison 1999; Longley 2001; Rippon in press).

Establishing a chronology and the role of schematic modelling

Within any area of countryside there will be features of different date and historic landscape analysis can help establish both a relative chronology and an absolute chronology for these phases of development. The example of the railway line and sea wall postdating the rest of the historic landscape on the Caldicot Level represents

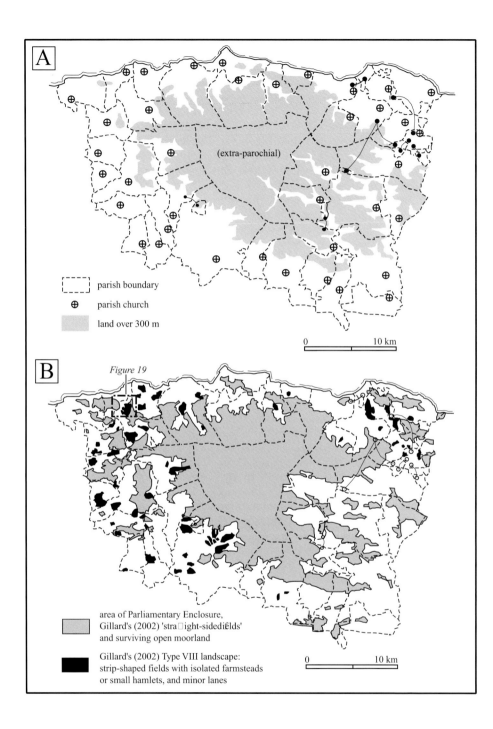

A

- - - - parish boundary

⊕   parish church

    land over 300 m

(extra-parochial)

0   10 km

B

Figure 19

    area of Parliamentary Enclosure,
Gillard's (2002) 'straⅡight-sidediÐlds'
and surviving open moorland

    Gillard's (2002) Type VIII landscape:
strip-shaped fields with isolated farmsteads
or small hamlets, and minor lanes

0   10 km

82

landscape stratigraphy. Other examples include the Grand Junction canal slicing through the ridge and furrow and post-enclosure fields in Bradwell (Fig 7), the medieval fields at Holne Moor overlying the Bronze Age reaves (Figs 13.1–2), and the railway line cutting across Hadleigh Marshes (Fig 15.2). Other examples of landscape stratigraphy are more subtle, such as the sequence of enclosures from Heale Down shown in Figure 19. The overall pattern of field boundaries, their relationship to the major earthen banks (eg the junction between the block of fields called 'Holland' and 'Higher Close' to the north), the clustering of field-names, and patterns of landownership as recorded in the Tithe Survey, together suggest a sequence of intakes starting with the block of long narrow fields including Bean Garden and Wheat Park, followed by the intake which included Gratton, then Holland, and then the block of fields to the north (Gillard 2002, figs 6.2, 6.10–13).

The chronology of different historic landscape components and types can also be enlightened by identifying when they are first **documented**. The historical record is very fragmentary and landscape features can go undocumented for many centuries, but even in moderately well documented areas there may be some correlation between different landscape types and when those features were first documented. Figure 3 (top) (see p 2), for example, shows a very distinctive type of landscape, which is consistently associated with settlements recorded in the Domesday Book; since this is the first comprehensive documentary source for this area all we can say is that the essential components of that landscape existed *by* 1066. Figure 3 (bottom) shows a very different landscape where no settlements are recorded before the 19th century.

The evolution of a particular historic landscape can be established firstly, through the use of stratigraphic and typological principles to establish a relative sequence for the evolution of a landscape, secondly through the attributing of some absolute date ranges through the identification of certain features in documentary sources, and thirdly, by drawing analogies with other, better documented/dated areas. In addition to this strongly empirical approach, schematic models can be drawn up to show in a general way how a particular landscape evolved. Such analysis has been applied before to particular landscape components such as settlements and field systems (eg Taylor 1975; 1983; Dodgson 1980; Unwin 1983; 1988; Roberts 1987; Roberts and Wrathmell 2002;), but there is also scope for modelling complete landscapes (see the marshland colonisation case study below).

Finally, there is a desperate need for the hypotheses generated by historic landscape analysis to be tested through **fieldwork**, and where this has occurred the

---

Figure 18: A: Greater Exmoor: the configuration of parishes radiating out from the extra-parochial area of the former royal forest of Exmoor so embracing a range of resources (after Gillard 2002, fig 2.5; redrawn by the author) B: two-fold division of the of the landscape of Greater Exmoor between firstly those areas surviving open moorland, Parliamentary Enclosure of former common, and other areas of morphologically very similar straight-sided fields suggestive of 17th-century or possibly later 'enclosure by agreement' (Whyte 2000, 83), and secondly, the remaining areas of 'ancient enclosure'. The identification of relatively recent areas of enclosure at an early stage of historic landscape analysis allows attention to then focus on those older landscapes of greater complexity. The area of 'ancient enclosure', for example, can be subdivided into eight types of which here Type VIII is highlighted (after Gillard 2002, figs 2.5, 5.5 and 5.39; redrawn by the author)

results are encouraging. A few examples must suffice. In Cornwall, for example, a Romano-British or earlier origin for the distinctive landscape of West Penwith has been confirmed through the excavation of field boundaries (Herring 1993; 1998, 63). On the Polden Hills in Somerset, a late prehistoric date has been confirmed for at least one of a series of long sinuous boundaries (M Aston and C Gerrard pers comm). The principles of landscape stratigraphy outlined above suggested that these boundaries predate the subdivision of the area into a series of manors recorded in Domesday, and indeed the laying out of a series of open field systems associated with the planned nucleated villages around the 10th century.

Figure 19: A: the hamlet of Heal in Parracombe parish, in the north-west fringes of Exmoor. Note the blocks of long, narrow, curving fields around the four farmsteads in Heale (Gillard's type VIII landscape). The analysis of Tithe Survey field-names allows the extent of woodland, the former common of Heale Down, and the steeper-sided slopes (denoted by '-cleave' names) to be identified. Several other clusters of field-names are suggestive of individual enclosures from the moor: 'Park' is a characteristic Devon and Cornwall field-name derived from Old English 'pearroc' meaning an 'enclosed piece of land' (Field 1993, 25), and in Parracombe they show a marked tendency to cluster around the medieval farmsteads and hamlets; Gratton is another common Devon field-name which Glover et al (1931, 28) suggest means 'stubble field' indicating arable cultivation (after Wainwright 2002). Other indicators of former arable cultivation include 'Bean Garden' and 'Wheat Park' (after Wainwright 2002). Field survey by Gillard (2002) showed that several of the earthen banks that appeared to define coherent blocks of fields (eg Gratton, Holland), and which presumably represent discrete intakes from formerly common land, were indeed larger than average (drawing: the author) B: The mid-19th century ownership of land in Heale was split between four tenements. landholdings in the blocks of long, narrow, and often curving fields close to the hamlet was scattered, whereas beyond what was presumably the earliest, open, field system there were discrete blocks of land held in severalty which presumably represent private intakes from open land such as 'Newer Parks' (Gillard 2002, fig 6.10; redrawn by the author)

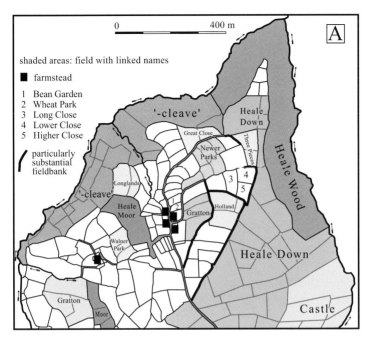

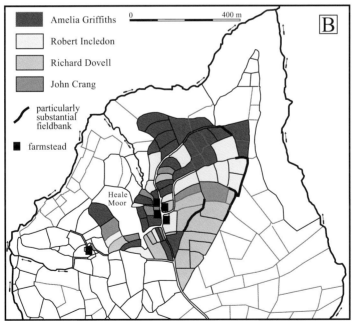

85

Figure 20: The Caldicot Level, South-East Wales: aerial view looking north-west from above the Severn Estuary. The 'irregular landscape' around Redwick lies at the centre with the area of 'intermediate landscape' created through the enclosure of the former open field at Broadmead to the left. The modern Llanwern Steelworks (now closed down) occupies the lower-backfen of the Caldicot Level (photo: the author)

CASE STUDY: THE EARLY STAGES OF MARSHLAND COLONISATION: PUXTON AND THE CALDICOT LEVEL (FIGS 17, 20, AND 22–4)

Key features:

- *regional-scale*
- *primary objective historical research, integrating archaeological and documentary sources*
- *explores the role of schematic modelling, and its testing through fieldwork, in order to increase our understanding of one of the physical processes behind the evolution of historic landscapes: the reclamation of wetlands*
- *further reading: Rippon 1996; 1997; 1999; 2000.*

Background

Since the 1980s the author has been researching historic landscapes created through wetland reclamation around the Severn Estuary. Over the years, a series of detailed local studies led to the realisation that very similar processes of marshland colonisation appear to have been going on all around the estuary, with a notable feature of the earliest phase of colonisation being roughly oval-shaped enclosures which were given the name 'infields' (eg Figs 24–5). Analysis of the historic landscape showed that such features are found on all the higher, coastal areas of marshland around the estuary and that they appeared to predate the immediately surrounding field boundary patterns. A key issue, however, was when in the evolution of these historic landscapes the 'infield' enclosures were created, and following Taylor's (1989b) seminal lead in self-reflection, the following case study will show how the generation, contemplation, testing, and revision of schematic models derived from historic landscape analysis can be an important part of the research process.

The natural environment

The Caldicot Level is an area of reclaimed coastal wetland in south-east Wales (Fig 20). Whilst appearing flat, like all wetlands it does have significant topographical variation, with slightly higher ground lying towards the coast since this is the area most often flooded by the tides, and so where most sediment is deposited (Fig 21.A). The higher coastal zone is crossed by a network of tidal creeks that drained the marshes at low tide, and which were often fossilised within the later historic landscape when they were used as field boundaries (Fig 21.B). A second set of natural watercourses are the rivers and streams that flow off the adjacent dryland areas and cross the marshes before discharging their water into the estuary; these were commonly canalised following reclamation to avoid the freshwaters from flooding the reclaimed lands (Fig 21.G).

The historic landscape

The key historic landscape components of field systems, settlements, commons, and roads/droveways, along with a relict landscape component, ridge and furrow, are shown on Figs 17 and 21. In terms of the landscape as it was mapped in the later 19th century (Fig 21.C–G), a series of broad historic landscape types can be identified (Fig 21.H):

- Parliamentary Enclosure: towards the eastern end of the Level lies an area of carefully planned mostly square fields, laid out between a grid of long, straight, narrow roads, resulting from the Parliamentary Enclosure of Caldicot Moor. This area has never been settled.
- Gradual, piecemeal reclamation: to the east and west of Caldicot Moor, on the higher coastal marshland, the landscape is mostly characterised by irregularly arranged field boundary patterns and sinuous roads, droveways, and commons that appear to respect (ie postdate) the 'infield' enclosures which became the focus for loosely nucleated settlements. Settled by the late 11th century. The inland limit of this landscape character type is often marked by long sinuous boundaries marking the former line of 'fen banks' designed to stop flooding by freshwater run-off in the backfens.
- Early enclosure of the backfens: between the coastal areas with their highly irregular layout, and the lowest-lying backfens, lies a heterogeneous 'intermediate' zone of more regularly arranged fields and just the occasional isolated farm and cottage. Several discrete blocks of landscape were created by the 13th century (eg

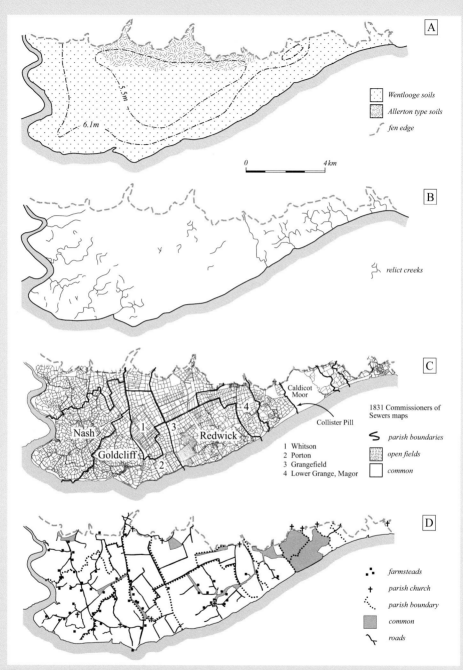

Figure 21: Caldicot Level: historic landscape components and types (drawn by Mike Rouillard) A: relief/soils; B: relict saltmarsh creeks (fossilised within the later field boundary pattern); C: field boundary pattern in 1831; D: settlement pattern.

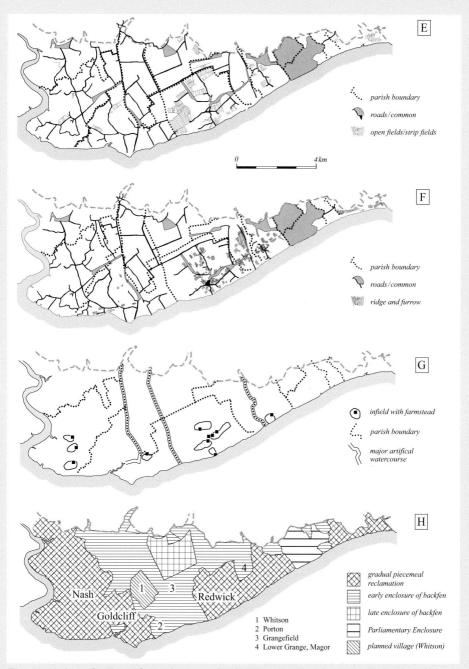

Figure 21 (contd): E: evidence for open fields; F: ridge and furrow; G: major embanked artificial watercourses carrying upland streams across the Levels, and 'infield' enclosures; H: historic landscape character types

89

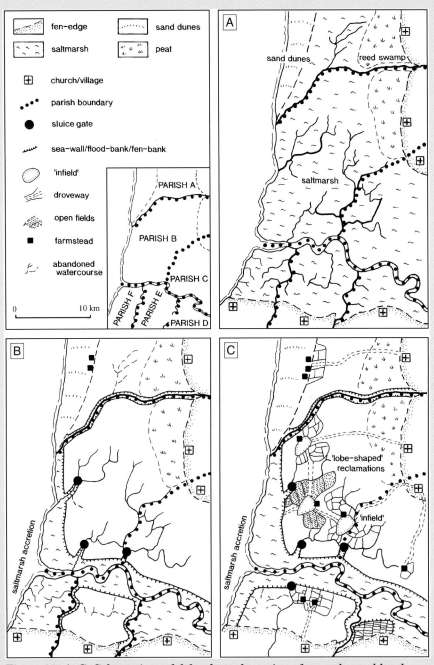

Figure 22: A–G: Schematic model for the reclamation of coastal marshland around the Severn Estuary, in south-west Britain (Rippon 1997a, fig 7)

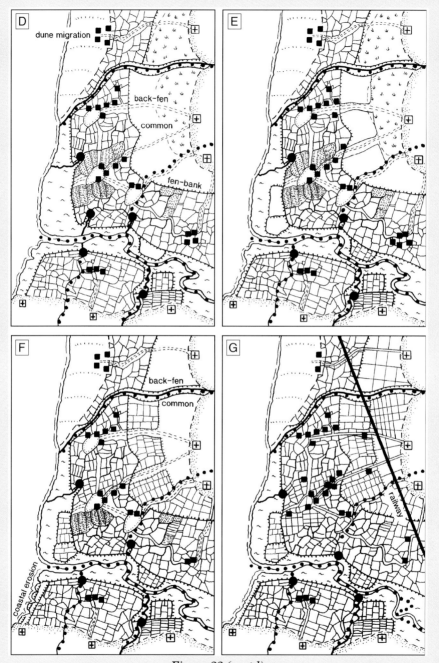

Figure 22 (contd)

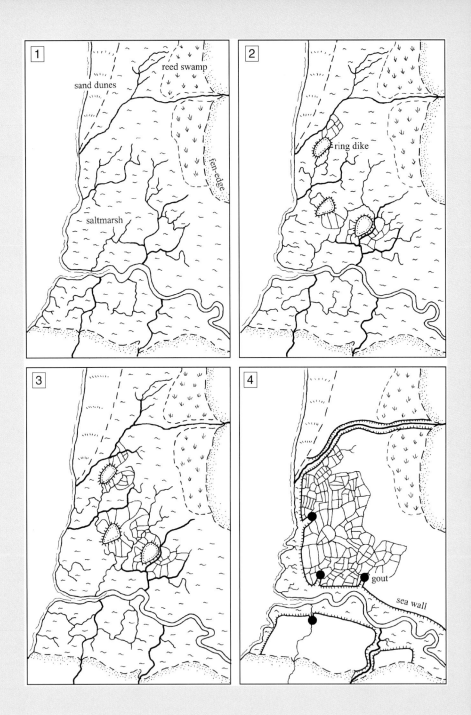

Grangefield, Lower Grange, and Porton), while elsewhere this landscape type was probably still being created into the early post-medieval period. A number of long straight boundaries appear to mark the line of former 'fen banks'.

- Late enclosure of the backfens: the lowest-lying backfens are characterized by very regular arrangements of rectangular fields, often laid out between long straight roads. This area has never been settled.
- Planned village: towards the centre of the Level lies a unique block of landscape, comprising a planned single-row village (Whitson) next to a funnel-shaped droveway/common (Fig 1).

A social context for historic landscape character

Part One of this handbook introduced the idea that the same type of countryside could have a very different character because in the past human communities/individuals decided upon different approaches towards exploiting that environment. A fundamental feature in the history of the Caldicot Level was Collister Pill which marks the western edge of Caldicot Moor as well as the boundary between two lordships established after the Norman Conquest (Fig 21 C). This provided the tenurial context within which the historic landscape was created. The lordships were Strigoil to the east (ie the unreclaimed Caldicot Moor) and Caerleon to the west (ie the embanked area of marshland around Redwick, Whitson, Goldcliff, and Nash). In the case of the Lordship of Caerleon, the decision to embark upon reclamation and colonisation appears to have been part of the wider Anglo-Norman policy of actively improving the productivity of their newly acquired estates, and the management of the landscape around Redwick in particular had a very 'English' feel: this is evident in the loosely nucleated green-side village with its extensive evidence for open fields, the single-row planned village at Whitson, and the almost uniformly English place-, field-, and personal names both today and in medieval documents. This contrasts sharply with another area of reclaimed marshland, the Wentlooge Level, immediately to the west, where place-, field-, and personal names were predominantly Welsh, settlement was largely dispersed and there is almost no evidence for open fields. As in Pembrokeshire, the landscape of the Redwick area appears to have been the product of English colonisation, whereas the Wentlooge Level reflects the indigenous Welsh approach to landscape management.

Understanding the early stages of marshland colonisation

Very similar landscapes to that of Redwick are found on reclaimed coastal wetlands on the English side of the Estuary. That there was a fundamental similarity in the process of wetland reclamation and historic landscape character all around the Severn

Figure 22 (contd): 1–4: Revised schematic model for the early phase of reclamation of coastal marshland around the Severn Estuary, in south-west Britain following contemplation, further data collection and revision of the original model (Rippon 2000a, fig 51; 2001, fig 6.1)

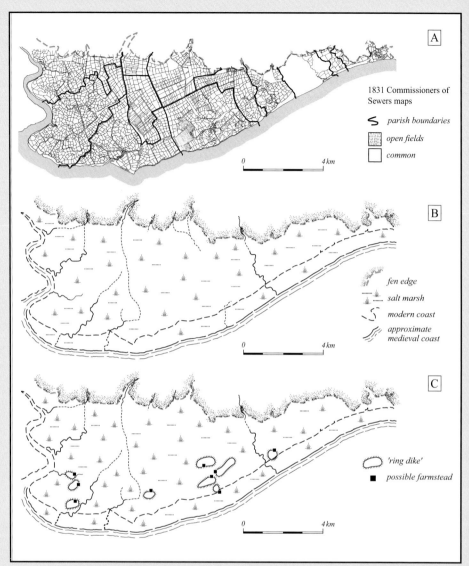

Figure 23: Revised model for the evolution of the historic landscape on the Caldicot Level, reflecting ideas since the initial publication of this research notably on the early phases of colonisation (after Rippon 1996a, fig 4; 2000d, fig 4; 2002, fig 1b). Note that the medieval coastline lay some 800 m to the south of the present sea wall (Rippon 2000d; Allen 2002): A: landscape in 1831; B: intertidal saltmarsh, traversed by tidal creeks and streams flowing off the adjacent uplands; C: initial colonisation through the construction of summer 'ring dikes'.

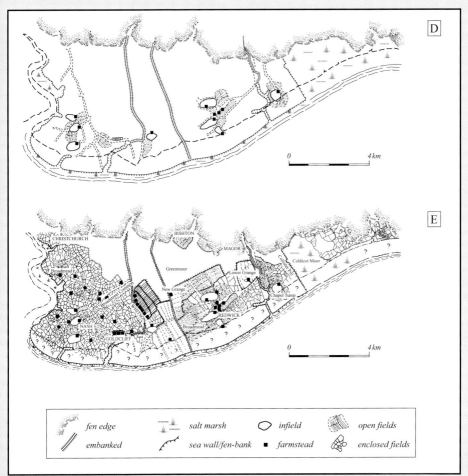

Figure 23 (contd): D: reclamation – construction of sea wall along the coast, embankment of the streams flowing off the uplands, and expansion of ditched field systems beyond the 'ring dikes'; E: enclosure and drainage of higher coastal areas, and construction of fen-banks at the edge of the backfen to prevent freshwater flooding. Note the extensive open fields and more nucleated settlement pattern of Redwick compared to Nash to the west (redrawn by Mike Rouillard)

Estuary was first observed by the author in his thesis *Landscape Evolution and Wetland Reclamation Around the Severn Estuary* (Rippon 1993). The Gwent Levels Historic Landscape Study led to an initial, and with hindsight rather crude, attempt to model the process of reclamation that could be inferred from the historic landscape (Rippon 1996a, fig 4), though publication of an estuary-wide overview gave the opportunity to improve upon this model (Fig 22 A–G: Rippon 1997a, fig 7). A key feature in the earliest phase of marshland colonisation was clearly the stratigraphically early 'infield' enclosures, which a programme of earthwork survey, fieldwalking, soil

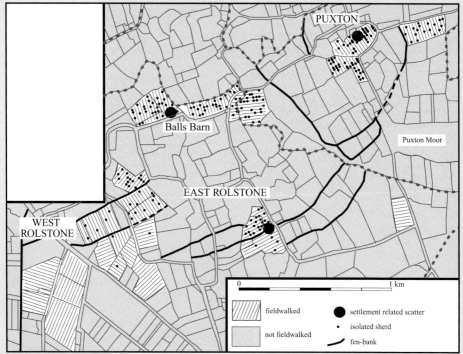

Figure 24: Puxton and Rolstone, on the North Somerset Levels. A series of long, sinuous boundaries would appear to be fen-banks designed to prevent freshwater flooding of the enclosed lands (to the north) from the lower-lying, unenclosed backfens (to the south). Fieldwalking showed that pottery scatters suggestive of manuring were largely to the north of these putative fen-banks (drawing: the author)

chemistry, and excavation at a number of sites has established were manured agricultural areas; they were not enclosed settlements, though a recurrent pattern was for one or more farmsteads to occur on the edge or just outside the enclosure (Figs 24–5; Rippon 1999b; 2001; 2002). The oval shape of these 'infields' suggests that they were created in an open landscape without other features to constrain their shape (woodland and moorland assarts similarly often take an oval shape: eg Holne Moor, Dartmoor: Fig 13). The question was: were the 'infields' created on an open saltmarsh or did they postdate the construction of a sea wall along the coast?

The initial model assumed that the first act on the part of those individuals and/or communities wishing to colonise these marshes was to construct a sea wall along the coast. After all, these landscapes are only sustainable today because of the massive embankments that protect them from tidal inundation. This was mistake number one: the natural environment is not constant, and in fact the mean sea level in the Severn Estuary during the medieval period was *c* 0.9 m lower than today, meaning that the flood defences could have been on a significantly smaller scale (Rippon 2002, 63). The assumption that the sea wall had to come first led inexorably to another, potentially erroneous, assumption: that the oval-shaped 'infield' enclosures had to

Figure 25: Puxton, on the North Somerset Levels, looking west. The oval 'infield' enclosure lies to the south of a small hamlet. A roughly concentric 'fen-bank' can be seen on the far left (photo: the author)

follow the construction of the sea wall. After all, who would live on a saltmarsh? This was mistake number two: we should not judge landscape potential through 21st-century eyes. Medieval communities may have had a higher tolerance of occasional flooding as a price worth paying for avoiding the costs of reclamation, and experiments with growing crops on mature saltmarshes, and palaeoenvironmental assemblages from both Britain and the continent, have shown that this was certainly done in the past (Rippon 2000a, 46–7).

A final stimulus leading to a revision of the model regarding the early stages of the reclamation came during a trip to the Netherlands, where the author became aware of a tradition of constructing 'summer dikes' on very high saltmarshes that were only flooded at the highest tides. These 'summer dikes', also known as 'ring dikes', were low embankments designed to protect an area of meadow or crops from unseasonally high summer flooding, but which made no effort to keep back the higher winter tides. This represented an alternative approach by human communities to the utilization of marshland landscapes. Rather than transforming them through reclamation, they could simply modify them through the construction of summer dikes to make a small area more suitable for growing crops. The building of a sea wall along the coast came later. This realization led the author to present an alternative schematic model for the initial stages in the creation of the historic landscape in coastal wetlands, with the oval-shaped 'infield' enclosures predating the construction of the sea wall along the coast (Fig 22, 1–4; Rippon 2000a, fig 51). This in turn led to the presentation of an alternative more detailed model for how the historic landscape of the Caldicot Level may have evolved (Fig 23: Rippon 2000d, 152–8, fig 4).

The hypothesis that the 'infield' enclosures were in fact 'summer dikes' has also been tested through fieldwork on the North Somerset Levels at Puxton (Figs 23–4; for location see Fig 27.2). Here excavation has shown that the 'infield' enclosure was indeed surrounded by a bank. Its enormous breadth (c 13 m) and very shallow angle suggest that it was designed to limit erosion, and so it would appear that these 'infield' enclosures were indeed summer ring dikes built on an active intertidal saltmarsh (this 'hypothesis' has now been confirmed by palaeoenvironmental analysis and soil micromorphology). The revised model of the early phases of marshland colonisation appears to be correct (Rippon 1999b; 2002; in press; Rippon et al 2001). The fieldwork in and around Puxton has allowed another hypothesis from the historic landscape analysis to be tested. To the south-west of Puxton, in East and West Rolstone, a series of long sinuous boundaries are suggestive of the lines of former fen-banks designed to prevent flooding of the enclosed lands to the north by freshwater run-off in the lower-lying unenclosed backfens to the south. Fieldwalking supports this hypothesis as light manure scatters of medieval pottery only occur in field to the north of the putative fen-banks (Fig 25).

SUMMARY SO FAR

- the term '**historic landscape**' was created in the 1990s to demonstrate to planners and countryside managers the time-depth present in our countryside (the '**future-oriented**' approach), and stress the value of studying the present pattern of fields, roads, settlements etc in academic research in the origins and development of the landscape (the '**past-oriented**' approach).

- the two broad approaches are '**bottom-up**', where every parcel of the landscape is assigned a particular set of characteristics and then this data is simplified in order to produce more generalised blocks of historic landscape character, and '**top-down**' where these generalised blocks are identified straight away, usually through existing professional knowledge of the area.

- in **England**, English Heritage are sponsoring a series of county-based future-oriented, bottom-up Historic Landscape Characterisation Projects which attribute all areas of landscape to one of a range of pre-determined types/zones.

- in **Scotland**, Historic Scotland and the Royal Commission on the Ancient and Historical Monuments of Scotland are similarly carrying out an on-going countrywide programme future-oriented, bottom-up Historic Landuse Assessment that follows a broadly similar approach.

- in **Wales**, Cadw and the Countryside Council for Wales have adopted a different approach, creating a selective *Register of Landscapes of Historic Interest in Wales* through a top-down process of consultation. This has identified the most important historic landscapes in Wales, and detailed Historic Landscape Characterisations are now being carried out for each in order to identify character areas, starting with The Gwent Levels Historic Landscape Study.

- **local knowledge** of the landscape and its archaeology and history, as well as understanding of the HLC/HLA techniques, is essential in a successful project.

- as a **research tool** historic landscape analysis is a means of **integrating** a wide range of source material relating to the origins and development of the historic landscape.

- it can be used at a variety of **scales**. For studies of relatively small areas, the earliest large-scale sources such as Tithe Maps should be used. When studying larger areas these are impractical and the best source is the First Edition Ordnance Survey Six Inch Series that provides the earliest comprehensive coverage of the British landscape at a level of detail to include field boundary patterns.

- for those new to landscape archaeology/history, the process of **retrogressive analysis** is a useful means of understanding the processes of landscape evolution.

- the historic landscape was created by human communities and understanding socio-economic factors are crucial to understanding why its character varies so much. Such factors include general phenomena like population levels and economic development, but also patterns of **landownership** that can be mapped, at least for the 19th century, as part of historic landscape analysis.

- the morphology of a historic landscape can be suggestive of its **date of origin**, and the creation of **schematic models** can help make sense of what are usually complex palimpsests. Such hypotheses can be **tested** through documentary research and archaeological fieldwork.

PART THREE
APPLICATIONS AND USES

SOME USES OF HLC IN PLANNING AND COUNTRYSIDE MANAGEMENT

In the 'future-oriented' world of planning and countryside management Historic Landscape Characterisation and Historic Landuse Assessment can be used in a number of ways:

Landscape Character Assessment

- The Countryside Agency has already published guidance on Landscape Character Assessment and the limited significance of time-depth and historical process is discussed in Part One. The on-going programme of HLC in England and HLA in Scotland is, therefore, essential as the importance of historic landscape character is otherwise so poorly addressed in Landscape Character Assessment.

Planning

- informing development plan policies at strategic (regional and structure plan) and local level
- informing studies of development potential, for example to help in finding sites for new development, both within or on the edge of towns, and in the wider countryside
- informing the design conditions for particular forms of development such as housing, minerals, and wind energy
- providing an input to Environmental Assessment for individual development proposals.

Landscape conservation, management, and enhancement

- informing the preparation of landscape management strategies
- helping to guide landuse change in positive and sustainable ways, for example programmes of woodland expansion, and new uses for disturbed and degraded land
- informing the targeting of agri-environment schemes.

In Part Three of this handbook some examples of historic landscape analysis and the uses to which it has been put are explored through a series of case studies. The first two are English Heritage sponsored county-based projects in Cornwall and Lancashire whose results have been widely published, allowing the reader to explore them further. The third case study is of the county of Somerset (in its pre-1974 form), taking one result of another English Heritage sponsored HLC project – revealing the possible extent of former open field farming – and exploring this further in order to show how regional variation in historic landscape character can be explored at a county scale. Alongside the case studies earlier in the handbook, these are intended to show the benefits of both analysing the historic landscape, and using existing HLC/ HLAs for research. Finally there is a parish-based case study, of Meare in Somerset, where the historic landscape is broken down into a series of discrete historic landscape areas, the evolution of which is enlightened through relatively extensive documentary sources.

CORNWALL – THE PRINCIPLES ESTABLISHED

Key features:
* *the first English Heritage sponsored HLC*
* *county-scale HLC designed to inform planners and countryside managers*
* *paper-based 'bottom-up' methodology ascribing every parcel of landscape to one of a series of predetermined landscape types based upon an interpretation of the major historical process(es) that contributed to that land parcel acquiring its present characteristics*
* *a straightforward product making high level generalisations (notably the simplification of types into zones)*
* *carried out by staff of the local archaeological unit (then part of the County Council Planning Department), with an excellent local knowledge of the landscape and a long history of actively researching its archaeology/history*
* *has seen a wide range of applications and further refinements of the methodology*
* *further reading:* Herring 1998.

The methodology

Cornwall was the first English county to be subject to HLC, and as such set the methodological agenda. In 1993 (as The Gwent Levels Historic Landscape Study started in Wales) the Cornwall Archaeological Unit (CAU) developed a methodology for assessing historic landscape character within the Bodmin Moor Area of Outstanding Natural Beauty (Countryside Commission 1994a; 1994b). In 1994, the CAU and Landscape Design Associates were appointed by the Countryside Commission and English Heritage to develop a methodology for assessing historic landscape character at a county scale (Cornwall County Council 1994; Herring 1998; 1999; Johnson 1999). This work built on a long history of both detailed and wide-ranging landscape work that is essential to a successful project. The Cornwall HLC followed two stages:

1. the attributing of each land parcel (ie field etc) to one of a series of generic descriptive 'historic landscape character **types**'

* Rough ground
* Prehistoric enclosures [field systems]

101

- Medieval enclosures
- Post-medieval enclosures
- Modern enclosures
- Ancient woodland
- Plantations and scrub woodland
- Settlement (historic)
- Settlement (modern)
- Industrial (relict)
- Industrial (active)
- Communications
- Recreation
- Military
- Ornamental
- Water (reservoirs etc)
- Water (natural bodies)

Predating the widespread use of GIS systems, this first county-based HLC project was carried out on paper, colouring in each historic landscape parcel.

2. These 'types' were then simplified and rationalised into a series of generic interpretative 'historic landscape character **zones**' in order to identify broader patterns each with a predominant historical landscape character derived from a historical process (Colour Plate A):

zones	*derivation from types*
Anciently enclosed land	amalgamation of 'prehistoric enclosures' and medieval enclosures' types
Upland rough ground	subdivision of the 'rough ground' type
Coastal rough ground	subdivision of the 'rough ground' type
Dunes	topographical subdivision of 'Rough Ground' type
Recently enclosed land	amalgamation of the 'post-medieval enclosures' and 'modern enclosures' types
Anciently enclosed land altered in the 18th and 19th centuries	interpretation of elements of prehistoric, medieval and post-medieval enclosures types
Anciently enclosed land altered in the 20th century	modern enclosures which are adaptations of prehistoric and medieval enclosures
Navigable rivers and creeks	topographic zone using OS maps as the principle source
Steep-sided valleys	topographic zone using OS maps as the principle source
Upland woods	subdivision of 'plantation and scrub woodland' type
Urban development	amalgamation of the 'settlement (historic)' and 'settlement (modern)' types
Predominantly industrial	amalgamation of the 'industrial (active)' and 'industrial (relict)' types
Military	simple derivation from 'military' type

zones	derivation from types
Ornamental	simple derivation from 'ornamental' type
Recreation	simple derivation from 'recreation' type
Reservoirs	simple derivation from 'water (artificial)' type
Intertidal zone	[no type]

For each landscape zone, and textual description was prepared based a standard format (see Table 3)

Subsequent refinements and research applications

The Cornwall HLC was the first of its kind and established that historic landscape character could be mapped at a county scale. Time was, however, limited, and in this early work the 'anciently enclosed land', which clearly covered a variety of field boundary patterns, was left undifferentiated (Herring 1998, 77–8). In what is an excellent demonstration of how HLC should not be allowed simply to gather dust, this important type has now been subdivided, and one project that contributed to this refinement – the Lynher Valley appraisal (Herring and Tapper 2002) – is also an excellent example of the use to which HLC can be put. In the late 1990s the Cornwall Farming and Wildlife Advisory Group, the Environment Agency, and the Cornwall Environmental Trust were increasingly concerned by the loss of soil from arable fields within the catchments of the rivers Lynher and Tiddy, and the effect of soil, chemical,

TABLE 3: Cornwall HLC – textual description for each zone (based on Herring 1999, 30–31)

Introduction	Basic defining or distinguishing attributes
Principal historical process	A brief review of the historical development of the zone in Cornwall, including an outline chronology where appropriate. Emphasis is laid on the processes (economic, social etc) that have produced surviving historical or semi-natural features.
Typical historical and archaeological components and features	Allows particular landscape features (like engine houses, church towers or conifer plantations) and below ground remains a place in the characterisation. Includes semi-natural habitats as well as archaeological features.
Rarity	A statement on the rarity regionally and nationally of both the zone itself and the features typically found within it in Cornwall.
Survival	A statement on the typical survival of historical/archaeological and semi-natural components and features within this zone in Cornwall. In some cases the survival of the whole zone is also considered.
Degree of surviving coherence	A statement on the typical extent that inter-related components from specified periods survive to be seen and understood in the zone.

103

TABLE 3 (contd)

Introduction	Basic defining or distinguishing attributes
Past interaction with other zones	A discussion of the apparent relationships between the zone under consideration and other zones at specific periods.
Evidence for time-depth	A discussion of the typical development of the zone (say 'Recently Enclosed Land developing on what was previously 'Upland Rough Ground', 'Ornamental' on 'Anciently Enclosed Land', or the gradual process of enclosure in 'Anciently Enclosed Land'), and the typical survival of visible and coherent evidence for that development.
Contribution to the present landscape character	Discussion of the extent that the historical/archaeological or semi-natural components that define the zone also determine the predominant landscape character of the land on which it lies.
Values and perception	A discussion of that ways that local people and visitors appear to perceive the zone and the value that is given to it and its components. Without the time to undertake a thorough literature search or conduct interviews, this was based on the observations and prejudices of one person who has lived in the county since a young child. This was an important part of the text, but bringing subjectivity into the process, and identifying variances in attitudes, and disputes over interpretations.
Research and documentation	Statement on the extent of archaeological and historical research on the development of both the zone and its typical components.
Potential for historical and archaeological research	Discussion of directions future research might take to help understand the development of both the zone itself and its components.
Potential for amenity and education	A discussion of the likely interest visitors and educators may find in the zone, its components, and its history, and the practical problems that might be encountered in developing that interest.
Condition	Statement on the typical condition of the zone and defining components.
Vulnerability	Statement on the degree of statutory or customary protection the zone typically receives.
Forces for change	Discussion of the influences currently affecting the zone in Cornwall; these need not all be negative.
Importance	Using some of the foregoing sections as a guide, a statement is made on the importance regionally and nationally of both the zone and its typical components.
Principal locations	Simple statement concerning typical distribution of the zone through Cornwall, sometimes with a brief explanation.
Variability	Statement identifying major differences in extent and components of the zone in different parts of Cornwall, with brief explanations where appropriate.
Safeguarding the zone	Simple recommendations made in the light of foregoing sections with the intention of conserving the zone, its components, and its character.

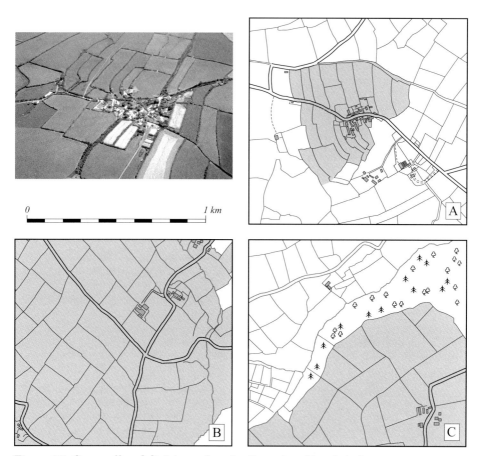

Figure 26: Cornwall: subdivisions of anciently enclosed land. A: long, narrow, curving fields, with dog-legs, that appear to represent the enclosure by agreement of former open field strips (with air photograph of an example: © Cornwall County Council); B: rectangular fields between long, sinuous boundaries, thought to represent the former cropping units/furlongs within open fields; C: large rectangular fields, often associated with 'Barton' place-names representing closes held in severalty (Based on Herring and Tapper 2002, fig 9–11 re-drawn by Mike Rouillard)

and nutrient inputs into the rivers and their tributaries. Cornwall Archaeological Unit was commissioned by the County Council to prepare a report on the historic environment to inform advice provided to farmers and landowners, to guide the targeting of agri-environmental schemes, and the design of other environmental programmes (eg the Environment Agency's run-off retarding schemes). Within the Lynher Valley project, HLC has also been used to raise the profile of the historic environment amongst the local community, including the promotion of more sustainable farming methods.

The Lynher Valley report was based on the original Cornwall HLC, though now the same characterisation was also applied to the landscape as mapped in the First Edition

Ordnance Survey Six Inch maps. An important development was that three distinctive subdivisions of the 'Anciently Enclosed Land' were recognised, the first two of which relate to a regionally distinctive form of farming known as 'convertible' or 'ley husbandry', whereby all the agricultural land of a particular farmstead or hamlet was divided between a series of 'cropping units' (Fig 26). Each cropping unit was surrounded by a stock-proof hedge bank, but could be subdivided into strips that were simply defined by a low bank; following the harvest all the strips in a particular cropping unit were grazing in common. A cropping unit would be cultivated for just two or three years and then put down to fallow for around six or seven years, producing a rotation in the order of nine to ten years (Hatcher 1970, 11–13; Jewell 1981).

Thus the first distinctive subdivision of the Cornwall HLC's 'Anciently Enclosed Land' is blocks of long narrow fields, often with marked dog-legs (Fig 26.1), which are very characteristic of the 'enclosure by agreement' of former open fields. These would appear to represent the cultivation strips within the former 'cropping units' of convertible husbandry. The second subdivision of 'Anciently Enclosed Land' is that of larger, roughly rectangular fields often with curving sides that represent these 'cropping units' themselves (Fig 26.2). A third subdivision is blocks of large, rectangular fields that morphologically are not dissimilar to post-medieval enclosures in the uplands (Fig 26.3). Place-names of the farmsteads associated with these blocks are often 'Home Farm' or 'Barton' suggesting that they represent former manorial demesne 'held in severalty' (ie managed by the lord himself, as opposed to being held by tenants).

This evidence contained within the fabric of the historic landscape is important as it provides virtually the only indication we have for the former extent of common-field farming in Cornwall. There is very little medieval documentary material for Cornish agriculture, and by the post-medieval period when records do survive, the landscape was enclosed. Convertible husbandry appears to have been restricted to Cornwall, Devon, and possibly the west of Somerset. Although it is well attested from the 15th century, a lack of good documentary material before that date makes its origins unclear (Harrison 1984, 370–1; Hatcher 1988, 387; Fox 1991). However, as an example of how archaeological techniques can be combined with historic landscape analysis, recent palaeoenvironmental work around the fringes of Exmoor, suggests an 8th–10th-century date for the onset of convertible husbandry in that area (Fyfe *et al* 2003; Fyfe *et al* in press) although an earlier date is possible in Cornwall (Turner 2003).

LANCASHIRE – A GIS-BASED APPROACH

Key features:

- *representative of the third generation of English Heritage sponsored HLCs*
- *county-scale HLC to inform planners and countryside managers*
- *fully GIS-based 'bottom-up' approach with each land parcel allocated to a defined 'polygon' with the same physical attributes based on field boundary morphology and/or a wide range of other functional landuses including woods, road and settlement patterns*
- *a mass of local detail can be manipulated within the GIS to produce a versatile product making high level generalisations based on the interpolated date and origin of each land parcel*

106

- *carried out by staff of the local County Council Planning Department, with a good local knowledge of the landscape and actively engaged in researching its archaeology/history*
- *further reading:* http://www.lancashire.gov.uk/environment/archaeology/lhlcp Darlington 2002; Ede with Darlington 2002.

The methodology

In common with other 'first generation' HLCs in England the mapping in Cornwall was on paper, and had a methodology based upon attributing each land parcel to one of a relatively limited series of predetermined thematic landscape types. The methodologies in subsequent English Heritage-funded county HLCs have developed this approach both in terms of the technologies used (notably computerised GIS systems), and the approach to classification. In common with the other English county-based HLCs, the Lancashire team was invited to develop its own methodology, which benefited from the experience of a number of other studies including the early application of GIS-based HLC in the Cotswolds and Hampshire. Darlington and Ede built on these to develop the approach further, and on similar lines to other contemporary projects such as that in Somerset.

The method began with the objective identification and description of historic attributes in each parcel of the modern rural and urban landscape. These attributes included 'all aspects of the natural and built environment that have been shaped by human activity in the past – the distribution of woodland and other semi-natural habitats, the form of fields and their boundaries, the lines of roads, streets and pathways, the disposition of buildings in the towns, villages and countryside' (Ede and Darlington 2002, 25). For the whole of the county the following attributes were examined (note that at this stage these attributes are wholly descriptive: the interpretation comes at a later stage):

- current landuse
- field shape
- field size
- field groups
- boundary types
- shape and disposition of paths/lanes/roads
- shape and type of woodland
- shape and type of water
- distribution and types of buildings
- contour/geology/soils
- place names
- settlement pattern
- previous fieldwork
- *c* 1850 mapping (Ordnance Survey First Edition Six Inch Series)
- enclosure awards and other historical information
- and, at the later assessment stage, SMR data.

Using these attributes, parcels were grouped into blocks ('polygons' in the GIS) sharing similar characteristics, and for each the following information was entered into the project database:

- **Polygon**: a unique identifier for each of the 4800+ polygons in the GIS
- **current landuse** of the polygon, including:
  - Enclosed land
  - Woodland
  - Recreational land
  - Communications
  - Coastal rough ground
  - Upland moor
  - Other unimproved land
  - Industrial land
  - Settlement
  - Ornamental land
  - Military
  - Water.
  Further subdivision was made on the basis of more specific landuses (for example dunes or saltmarsh within coastal rough ground), or on the basis of enclosure size or shape. The coding also included an element to indicate degree of change between the c 1850 First Edition Six Inch and the modern mapping.
- **former landuse:** (and shape and size) in c 1850, taken from the First Edition Six Inch mapping if different from the present day
- **Slope:** a field for identifying steep ground; only used in association with woodland categories
- **Pits:** a field for identifying the presence or absence of sand, marl or gravel pits in the enclosed land and other categories
- **Boundary:** a field for identifying water-filled boundary ditches in the enclosed land categories
- **Interpretation:** identifying origins of enclosed land (for example areas of current enclosed land which were previously mossland)
- **Date**: the date of the predominant historic character of the polygon
- **Confidence:** a field in which a combined measure of confidence is allocated to the date and interpretation fields
- **Comment:** a field for descriptive notes
- **Checked:** a field to confirm that the polygon has been double-checked by someone other than the Project Officer.

The primary attributes that dictated the extent and scale of subdivision were **current landuse** and **historic landuse**, with further subdivision made on the basis of enclosure size and shape. In this way areas of the same landuse were subdivided along morphological grounds. For example irregular wavy-edged fields were separated from areas of irregular straight-edged fields, or straight-edged plantations of woodland were split from tracts of irregularly bounded woodland. This methodology also allowed the interpretative elements of the mapping (ie predominant date of current landuse, or likely origins) to be distinguished from the purely descriptive.

Once each polygon had been described and digitised they were analysed and grouped under generic historic landscape character types that shared distinct attributes. For example, an area possessing a pattern of small, irregular fields, dissected by winding lanes and footpaths, associated with known medieval settlements, place- and field-names, and shown to be in existence prior to the earliest comprehensive map evidence may have been allocated to the 'Ancient Enclosure' (pre-AD1600) HLC type. The resulting mapping includes the following HLC types, each of which is accompanied by a detailed textual description (Colour Plate D1):

- Ancient (pre-AD1600) enclosure
- Post-medieval (AD1600–1850) enclosure
- Modern (post-AD1850) enclosure
- Ancient and post-medieval (pre-AD1850) woodland
- Modern woodland
- Ancient and post-medieval settlement
- Modern settlement
- Ancient and post-medieval industry
- Modern industry
- Ancient and post-medieval ornamental land
- Modern ornamental land
- Modern recreational land
- Modern military
- Modern communications
- Moorland
- Reverted moorland
- Lowland moss and grassland/scrub
- Water
- Coastal rough ground
- Saltmarsh
- Dunes
- Sand and mudflats.

Discussion and examples of analysis

The GIS-based Lancashire HLC can be interrogated in various ways. The analysis shows, for example, that not surprisingly 'Ancient Enclosure' (pre-AD 1600) concentrates in the lowlands, with a subsequent expansion of agriculture into both the low-lying wetlands and higher uplands during the post-medieval period (Colour Plate D2). 'Enclosed land' is the most extensive historic landscape type in the county, being used mainly for grazing sheep and cattle. As with all agricultural areas, 'the type has a significant impact on aspects of the social and cultural life of the county, where both its form and maintenance are defining characteristics of the aesthetic appeal of the landscape, and is in turn a major influence upon matters such as tourism and planning' (Ede and Darlington 2002, 92). 'Ancient enclosure' accounts for 39% of enclosed land (25% of Lancashire as a whole), 'post-medieval enclosure' for 48% and 'modern enclosure' for 13%. Around 80% of both 'ancient' and 'post-medieval enclosure' types have changed little in the past 150 years, especially when compared with the 'modern enclosure' type which is largely the result of changes to a previously enclosed landscape (*ibid*). Most enclosure in Lancashire is irregular in layout. These patterns, coupled with their small size, point to enclosure by individual farmers for their own use or by the agreement of small communities over a long period of time. It is typical of Rackham's (1986) 'ancient countryside' (see Part One above), a landscape of hamlets and dispersed settlements, of irregular ancient woodland, and a complex pattern of footpaths and roads. It is a landscape of intricacy and diversity rather than uniformity and plan.

One of the HLC interpretative attribute tags for each land parcel attempted to identify the origins of enclosure (Colour Plate D3). When plotted, this shows a clear distinction between the east and the west of the county which is entirely influenced by topography, with enclosure from mossland (peat bogs) in the lowland west, and enclosure from upland moor and woodland in the east on the fringes of the remaining unenclosed uplands. Seven per cent of the 'ancient enclosure' type originated from the division of open fields, which remain in the landscape today either as fossil strip fields (with their boundaries usually formed by hedges; 3%), or as a distinctive pattern indicative of the enclosure of bundles of strips and other elements of the previously open field (4%) (Ede and Darlington 2002, 98–9).

As a planning-based HLC, a key feature of the work in Lancashire was making recommendations for enhancing and safeguarding each historic landscape type. The boxed case study below for the 'ancient and post-medieval industry' for example, gives its 'historic landscape character type' description and list of recommendations. This is followed by a more general overview, by Jo Clark of Lancashire County Council, of the diverse uses to which the English Heritage sponsored county-based HLCs have been put in informing planners and countryside managers of the time depth present within the historic landscape.

CASE STUDY: LANCASHIRE HLC TYPE: ANCIENT AND POST-MEDIEVAL INDUSTRY

General description

Historical and archaeological background and principal processes: **Ancient and Post-Medieval Industry** *covers 549 hectares of Lancashire. Of this 368 hectares (67%) comprise disued quarries. The bulk of the remainder (158 hectares or 29%) includes active quarries that were present on the First Edition mapping, although understandably their extent was often considerably smaller than that of today. Most of the quarries lie in east Lancashire where sources of sandstone were particularly important for roofing, paving and building material. There are also limestone quarries in the Silverdale and Kellet areas of north Lancashire and near Clitheroe.*

The mapping scale selected for the project precluded small areas of older industry. Consequently the evidence for rural textile milling and many smaller quarries still extant in the landscape are not included within the type. Instead these represent attributes of other HLC types, in particular **Settlement** and **Moorland**.

Time-depth can be visible in the active quarries where a chronology of quarry progress may be mapped within the landscape, particularly if that progress follows a specific seam of source material. In addition, older structures may be present within quarries, both in active and abandoned states.

Typical historical and archaeological components: *There are likely to be structures and features associated with different phases and processes of the relevant industry, for example limekilns in the limestone hushings of Burnley and Colne, or abandoned tramways and railways in the stone quarries of the Rossendale Valley. The features associated with this HLC type may abruptly interrupt older landscape elements such as previously existing tracks, banks, and field systems. The rock faces today may be valuable geological sites and protected as such as SSSIs or RIGs.*

Enhancing and safeguarding the type

- *Conserve* and *enhance* the remains of Lancashire's early industrial landscape. The industrial heritage of Lancashire remains one of the county's defining characteristics, providing instantly recognisable local distinctiveness for those living both in and outside of the county. Such heritage, particularly when measured against its international contribution, has much to offer that is unique and special to the county. Whilst much of this character is present as individual buildings and structures within other HLC types (especially **Settlement** and **Moorland**) the concentration of surviving or relic industry in the industrial type indicates a significant resource that may be retained for economic and social benefit as well as in its own right.

- *Pursue* opportunities for heritage-led regeneration in areas through tourism and sustainable reuse of key industrial buildings and areas. The *Heritage Conservation in Lancashire* strategy document provisionally identifies the following priority industrial landscape areas: Lancashire's textile and related heritage, and the quarry heritage of the Rossendale Valley. To this may be added the landscape of limestone hushings at Burnley and Colne, copper and ironworking areas in Silverdale, and the leadworking at Rimington and Anglezarke.

- *Ensure* that the historic dimension of industrial landscapes is properly assessed during proposals for change. Industrial landscapes are vulnerable to change both through neglect and through programmes of land reclamation. Initiatives such as quarry reclamation schemes, derelict land programmes (for example the REMADE in Lancashire programme and the Small Sites programme), contaminated land strategies and environmental improvement projects may all coincide with areas of former industrial heritage. These should be informed by appropriate levels of information in order that decisions can be made to conserve important assets, record others, and to ensure that the historic environment may act as a positive catalyst for change.

- *Increase* awareness of the historical basis and context for **ancient and post-medieval industry** landscapes in order to improve perception and appreciation. Priority will be given to establishing an inventory of textile working sites to match surveys already completed in Greater Manchester, West Yorkshire and Cheshire, and within the Pendle District, and to completing an audit of Rossendale quarry heritage.

Source: http://www.lancashire.gov.uk/environment/archaeology/lhlcp/3results4.pdf

CASE STUDY: USING HISTORIC LANDSCAPE CHARACTERISATION

by Jo Clark

Since its inception in Cornwall in 1994, the English Heritage sponsored Historic Landscape Characterisation (HLC) programme has brought large-scale characterisation into the field of heritage management, shifting objectives from the site specific to a consideration of the whole landscape. Over half of the country is now covered by HLC and it is being used with great success to advise and inform a large number of applications, which are predominantly rural in nature but increasingly urban as projects such as Lancashire and Merseyside extend characterisation into our towns and cities.

In 2002 Jo Clark and John Darlington of Lancashire County Council were commissioned by English Heritage to carry out a national review of the applications of Historic Landscape Characterisation. The review sought to identify where HLC was reaching it full potential, as well as where it was encountering barriers to use, as well as assessing how these might be overcome. From this work a booklet providing an introduction to the principles of HLC, including application case studies that demonstrate best practice has been produced called *Using Historic Landscape Characterisation*, which discusses the use of HLC under the following application areas:

Landscape Management

HLC has a well-established track record of being used to advise agri-environment schemes across England and its value as a vital source of information about the historic landscape is appreciated by a range of officers. For example, HLC is used extensively by Historic Environment Countryside Advisors, particularly in Cornwall where well-established methods ensure that the needs of the historic environment are taken into full account when advising schemes. HLC has also been used to influence the targeting of Countryside Stewardship Schemes and Special Projects, such as the Axholme open fields project launched by DEFRA in 2003.

Landscape Character Assessments and Strategies

HLC has been used to define, understand and describe the types of numerous Landscape Character Assessments, and to inform landscape strategies. For example, in Lancashire the HLC was used to amend and redefine character types and the urban character types were adopted wholesale from the HLC mapping; while in Hampshire the countywide HLC has been used to inform district historic landscape assessments, which in turn, have been prepared in order to inform landscape character assessments.

Spatial Planning

Given the restrictions of the development plan cycle, the generation and inclusion of new policy is restricted. Despite this, there are a number of examples where HLC has been used to inform new planning policy and supplementary planning guidance (SPG), which recognise the value of the historic landscape as a whole, instead of the traditional approach of protecting isolated sites. This includes the Draft Herefordshire Unitary Development Plan (2002), Policy LA2 of which states:

> Proposals for new development that would adversely affect either the overall character of the landscape, as defined by the landscape character assessment and the historic landscape characterisation or its key attributes or features, will not be permitted.

HLC is regularly used to advise planning applications, as well as the assessment stages of major development schemes. It has been used in the assessment of the sensitivity of the London-Stansted-Cambridge Growth Area, which has been identified by the government as being an area that can help to meet the countries housing and economic needs over the next 20–30 years. Similar approaches are being developed for the Milton Keynes and the South Midlands, and the Thames Gateway Growth Areas.

Informing Other Work Areas

Initiatives that are built around the concept of character are making productive use of HLC, such as Conservation Area Appraisals, Parish Plans and Village Design

Schemes. Bath and North East Somerset Council have extended the area of the existing Conservation Area of Chew Magna to take into account the historic landscape character of the immediately surrounding area.

Increasingly HLC is being recognised as a useful method of integrating information about the historic landscape into management plans, for example at Cotehele House in Cornwall that has been the subject of a large scale HLC commissioned by the National Trust, and which has placed the property in its landscape context, improved understanding and enhanced presentation. Also, the historic environment section of the Forest of Bowland AONB Management Plan has been based on HLC.

Asking New Questions

A handful of local authorities have begun to explore the role of HLC in the field of research into the historic environment, in particular through providing context for SMR information. HLC is also taught at some universities, for example as part of heritage management degrees at York and Southampton, and the MA in Landscape Archaeology at Exeter.

The use of HLC for research purposes is discussed in much greater detail throughout this CBA handbook.

Access and Outreach

HLC is provided in a variety of formats – reports, mapping, Internet and CD ROM, to users and the community, helping to raise awareness of the historic landscape and start the difficult process of establishing the true community and democratic participation that the European Landscape Convention promotes.

Two reports can be viewed on-line

Hampshire: www.hants.gov.uk/landscape
Lancashire: www.lancashire.gov.uk/environment/archaeology/lhlcp/index.asp

The uses of HLC are steadily growing: in many ways it is still proving itself and in the coming years new applications will be revealed. There is a great deal of enthusiasm for HLC, and this is expected to increase as the initiative becomes better known and its applications better established. Local authorities have achieved a lot in a short space of time and the importance and function of HLC has been consolidated by the creation of an English Heritage Characterisation Team who are exploring its potential and helping to direct its path into the future.

Using the extent of former open/subdivided fields suggested by the HLC project as a starting point (Fig 27.1), this case study will illustrate how these 'future-oriented' projects can be taken forward through further research.

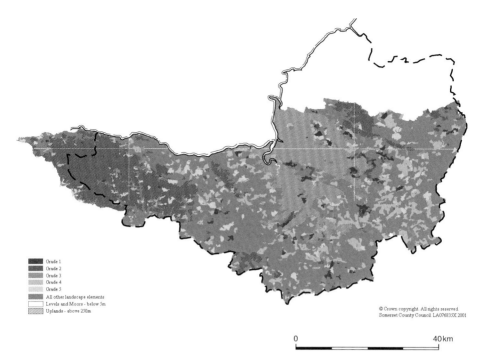

Figure 27.1: Somerset: extent of former common field, based on criteria such as field boundaries with a reversed-S curve, identified in the English Heritage sponsored HLC of the modern county of Somerset and Exmoor National Park (Aldred 2001, fig 16, appendix 4, © Somerset County Council). The historic county boundary has been added

SOMERSET – BEYOND HLC TOWARDS THE ORIGINS OF VILLAGES AND OPEN FIELDS

Key features:
- *takes a county-scale HLC as the starting point for research into the origins and development of the historic landscape in the context of research*
- *investigation of the role of the natural environment and socio-economic factors in shaping historic landscape character.*

The fundamental division in landscape character between the 'champion' and the 'woodland' regions of England was introduced in Part One, and this case study is a contribution to the long-running debate over how these marked regional variations came about. Somerset is an interesting county as it straddles the western limit of nucleated villages and open fields, which Rackham (1986), and Roberts and Wrathmell's (2000a) mapping of 19th-century settlement, draws along a line between the estuaries of the Axe on the Devon – Dorset border and the Parrett in Somerset. Somerset was the subject of an English Heritage-sponsored HLC (Aldred 2001; 2002) and this case study uses that as the starting point in considering the development of the county's broad

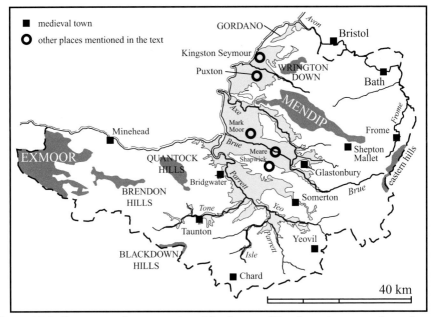

Figure 27.2: Somerset: places mentioned in the text. Note how the county boundary follows major uplands/watersheds to the west, south-west and east (drawing: the author)

character areas or *pays*. This is done by analysing and integrating a series of datasets relating to the natural environment, the physical fabric of the historic landscape, and the socio-economic and tenurial context within which it was exploited. Using the extent of former open/subdivided fields suggested by the HLC project as a starting point (Fig 27.1), this case study will illustrate how these 'future-oriented' projects can be taken forward through further research.

The physical landscape

Relief (Fig 27.2)
The physical topography of Somerset is extremely complex, ranging from low-lying wetlands through to a range of what until the 19th century were unoccupied uplands. This varied topography has had a profound effect on the origins and development of the historic landscape. Central and north-west Somerset are dominated by low-lying wetlands that are today protected from flooding by an extensive and complex system artificial embankments and drainage ditches. These wetlands are mostly fringed by gently undulating foothills which in the north lie in the shadow of the limestone up-lands of Mendip, Wrington Down, and the Failand Ridge, the highest parts of which were unenclosed common pasture in the medieval period. North-east of Mendip lie a series of limestone hills and clay vales around Bath and Bristol, while to the south-east of Mendip and the Levels lies the gently undulating lowland plain of south-east Somerset around Yeovil. To the west of the Somerset Levels lie the extensive gently

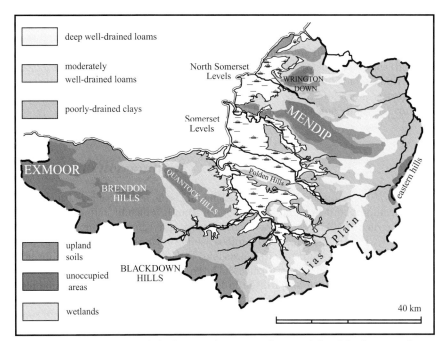

Figure 27.3: Somerset: simplified map of major soil types (after Mackney et al 1983; drawing: the author)

undulating lowlands around Taunton, Bridgwater, and Minehead, interrupted by the Quantock Hills and bounded to the west by the uplands of Exmoor and the Brendon Hills. The higher areas of all three of these uplands were unenclosed until the later post-medieval period.

Although many county boundaries bear little relationship to the wider landscape, those in Somerset did. The historic and indeed modern eastern, southern, and western boundaries of the county all lie close to major watersheds which were either only sparsely settled or unoccupied until the post-medieval period. Thus to the east lies the woodland-covered scarp of the eastern hills at Penselwood, while to the south lie the Blackdowns and associated hills west of Chard; to the west lies Exmoor.

Soils (Fig 27.3)

Even a cursory examination of a national soils map reveals that those in Somerset were extremely varied: nowhere are there extensive areas of relatively uniform soils such as the claylands of the Weald, East Anglia, and the Cheshire Plain, or the shallow chalky soils of Wessex (Mackney *et al* 1983). The uplands of Mendip, the Blackdown Hills, Quantocks, Brendon Hills, and lower parts of Exmoor typically have moderately deep to deep-loamy soils (Manod and Milford Series); the higher parts of Exmoor have waterlogged peaty soils (Larkbarrow Series). The lowlands of western Somerset (around Bridgwater, Minehead, and Taunton) are predominantly moderately well-drained loamy/clay-loam soils (Whimple Series). The lowland areas of western Somerset, the foothills surrounding the Somerset Levels, and parts of the lowland

117

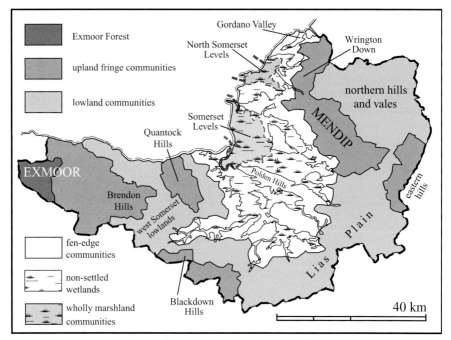

Figure 27.4: Somerset: major physical regions in terms of how human communities exploited the landscape during the historic period. Note that these do not simply follow divisions in the natural landscape as in 'interface areas' (eg upland fringe and wetland edge) because medieval estates straddled different environments (drawing: the author)

plain to the south (in the Taunton/Somerton/Castle Cary area) have a range of generally relatively poorly draining/slowly permeable clayey soils of the Denchworth, Evesham, Wickham, and Worcester Series, with areas of lighter soils of the Sherbourne Series on the higher areas (notably the Polden Hills and west of Somerton). In the south east, around Ilminster, Yeovil, and Castle Cary, lie further areas of moderately well drained loamy/clay-loam soils (Whimple Series) and well drained silty loams (Sherbourne and South Petherton Series); to the east, between Frome and Wincanton, lie further areas of heavier soils of the Denchworth and Evesham Series. The patterns of soils in the north-east of Somerset are particularly complex and varied, though they are predominantly moderately well drained loamy/clay-loam soils in the vales (notably the Whimple series) with areas of shallow well drained soils on the limestone hills (notably of the Sherbourne Series), with slowly permeable clayey soils of the Evesham Series predominating south of Bath.

The regions of Somerset from a socio-economic perspective (Fig 27.4)

The physical landscape of Somerset can be divided into four upland-related regions, three lowland-related regions, and three wetland and fen-edge related regions.

Traditionally these would have been based on criteria such as contours but the contention here is that this is not always a very helpful approach. In the evolution of the historic landscape, uplands and lowlands were linked via the key interface zones of the upland fringe and fen-edge. Thus, while some areas of the lowlands and wetlands were indeed sufficiently extensive to support communities whose territories (as reflected in parishes) were wholly within those topographies, and the uplands all had areas that were beyond the limits of medieval settlement and cultivation, large parts of Somerset lay within parishes that *straddled* these topographical zones.

Upland and upland fringe communities

- **Exmoor**: Exmoor dominates the western end of Somerset though only the far west actually lay beyond the limits of medieval cultivation/settlement. Its relatively extensive upland fringe fell within a series of large parishes that incorporated small areas of unenclosed land on the higher watersheds of the hills and ridges, with settlement/agricultural land in the intervening valleys. Exmoor's eastern outliers, the **Brendon** and **Quantock Hills**, fell within a series of large parishes radiating from those uplands.
- **Blackdowns and other southern Hills**: largely in Devon, the northern fringes of this upland extend a short distance into Somerset, being exploited from a series of adjacent lowland parishes.
- **eastern hills**: ridge/scarpland along the eastern boundary of Somerset lying within a series of large parishes whose centres lay on the edge of the adjacent lowlands.
- **Mendip**: limestone upland dominating northern Somerset, exploited from a series of large parishes around its periphery. The associated uplands of **Wrington Down** and the **Failand Ridge** lay to the north and similarly marked the boundaries between relatively large parishes.

Lowland communities

- **The west Somerset lowlands**: vales and gently undulating lowlands with good agricultural soils around Bridgwater, Minehead, and Taunton.
- **The Lias Plain (south-east Somerset)**: gently undulating lowlands in south-east Somerset with mixed generally good agricultural soils though with areas of impeded drainage.
- **The northern hills and vales**: sometimes steeply-sided limestone hills with gently undulating clayland vales, giving rise to mixed generally good agricultural soils with some areas of impeded drainage.

Wetlands and fen-edge communities

- **The Somerset Levels, North Somerset Levels and Vale of Gordano**: a mixture of higher, alluvial marshes towards the coast, freshwater peatbogs in the valleys either side of the Polden Ridge, and a series of alluvium-filled valleys leading into the Levels from the south and east. The coastal alluvium supported wholly marshland communities (often based upon small bedrock islands), while the

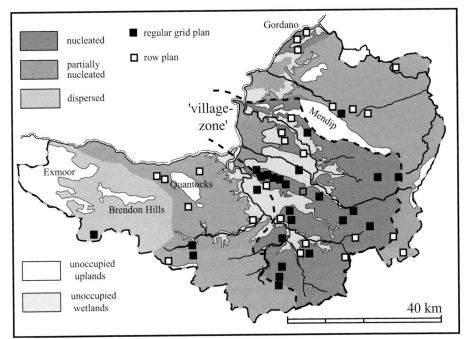

Figure 27.5: Somerset: 19th century settlement patterns (after Roberts and Wrathmell 2000a, fig 17). Note that Roberts and Wrathmell's 'Central Province' extends into western Somerset where a number of nucleated settlements lie in a landscape with a high degree of dispersion: in contrast, the 'village zone' is defined in this study as that part of Somerset where nucleated settlement was the dominant form of settlement within a parish (drawing: the author)

remaining areas were exploited by communities living close to the fen-edge and whose territories included both wetland and dryland. Figure 27.4 shows how these fen-edge communities, whose parishes extended across the non-settled areas of wetlands, dominated the central part of Somerset.

Settlement *(Fig 27.5)*

The 19th-century settlement pattern in Somerset ranged between almost wholly nucleated in the central and south-east regions, to almost wholly dispersed in the west (around Exmoor and the Brendon Hills). There was not a black and white divide between the nucleated and non-nucleated areas, but based upon Roberts and Wrathmell's (2000a) mapping the following settlement 'zones' can be identified:

- The main 'village zone' occupied south-east and central Somerset (and see Ellison 1983), along with an isolated area of wholly nucleated settlement around the Gordano Valley in the north-west of the county. In the far east of Somerset, settlement was (and still is) more dispersed.

120

- To the north of Mendip the settlement patterns were more mixed, with some nucleated villages, some areas with predominantly small hamlets, and other places where settlement was almost wholly dispersed.
- In central southern Somerset, the lowlands immediately west of the Parrett, and along the coastal zone of western Somerset, the settlement pattern was also mixed with some areas with predominantly small hamlets, and other places where settlement was almost wholly dispersed. Note that although Roberts and Wrathmell include these areas in their 'Central Province' the significant levels of dispersion should exclude them from the village-zone proper.
- In the far west of Somerset the landscape was dominated by the uplands of the Quantocks, Brendon Hills and Exmoor. Settlement on the fringes of these upland areas was almost wholly dispersed with isolated farmsteads and only occasional small agglomerations.

Field systems *(Figs 27.6–8)*

The historic landscape contains two distinctive signatures from open field farming. Piecemeal enclosure can lead to the fossilisation of strips as long narrow fields, with their distinctive curved boundaries, while Parliamentary Enclosure led to rigid, geometrically planned patterns of large rectilinear-square fields. Using such morphological criteria Aldred (2001, fig 16) has suggested that the distribution of open/subdivided fields extended across the whole of lowland Somerset, including areas west of the River Parrett that fall beyond the zone of nucleated villages (Fig 27.1). Was this really the case?

The extent to which open fields survived into the **late 18th/19th centuries** can be shown through the Parliamentary Enclosure Acts (Fig 27.6; Turner 1978). These show that the surviving open fields were almost wholly restricted to south-east and central Somerset, with a few outliers notably around the Gordano Valley in north-west Somerset (this significantly modifies the more general picture given by Gonner 1912, map A).

A comprehensive characterisation of pre-19th-century field systems is impossible and so the actual extent of open field agriculture in around 1300 is impossible to reconstruct. There are various sources, however, that give a general picture. Aston (1988d, fig 5.5) plotted the distribution of known open fields based on **medieval and early post-medieval documentary evidence**, including that published in the then available Victoria County Histories (Dunning 1974; 1981; 1985) and Whitfield's (1981) study of south-east Somerset. Aston's work can be updated through subsequent VCHs (Dunning 1992; 1999) alongside a number of other studies: Corcos' (2002) examination of Carhampton, Chew, and Whitley Hundreds; Gillard's (2002) work in the Greater Exmoor area; Musgrove's (1997; 1999; 2001) and Rippon's (1993, 1997a) research on the Somerset Levels and adjacent fen-edge manors; and Keil's (1964) study of the Glastonbury Abbey estates (Fig 27.7). The coverage of these studies is fairly good although the north-east and south-west remain under-represented. The pattern observed by Aston is confirmed, with places where there is evidence that open fields were absent being restricted to the very south and south-west of the county (Fig 27.7). Regular two-field systems dominated central and south-east Somerset, with three-fields systems concentrating in the central-south. Whilst there is clear evidence for

121

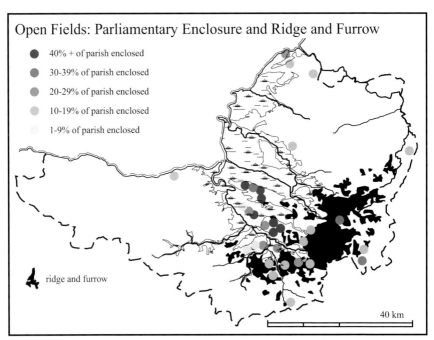

Figure 27.6: Somerset open fields: extent of Parliamentary Enclosure (after Turner 1978) and evidence for ridge and furrow (after Aston 1988d, fig 5.3) (drawing: the author)

common-field agriculture in the lowlands west of the Parrett, this was mainly in the coastal lowlands and was of a relatively small-scale and irregular nature (Fig 27.8); this was not the same as the Midland-style two- and three-fields systems of areas to the east. This is crucial in qualifying Aldred's results: morphology alone cannot be used to reconstruct past field systems. Gillard (2002), for example, has reconstructed the extent of some of these small open field systems, usually associated with a small hamlet of a handful of farmsteads, and shown that they typically covered 0.2–0.5 sq km (eg Heale, Exmoor: Fig 19) which is in contrast to the regular two- and three-field systems of the 'village zone' that covered virtually entire parishes (eg Bradwell, Buckinghamshire: Fig 7).

The distribution of regular open fields being restricted to central, southern, and south eastern Somerset as derived from documentary material is confirmed by the evidence from surviving **ridge and furrow** that is wholly restricted to the south and east of the county (Fig 27.6). This distribution will, however, reflect a number of factors: the creation of ridge and furrow in the first place through open-field farming, its survival due to a subsequent change in landuse (to pasture), and the visibility of now ploughed-out ridge and furrow through cropmarks.

Overall, therefore, the various indicators of former open fields suggests four broad 'zones' that, not surprisingly, match very closely the settlement patterns:

• The area of regular open fields (predominantly two-field systems) occupies south-east and central Somerset, along with an isolated area around the Gordano Valley

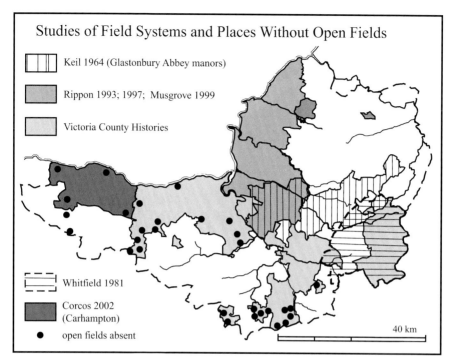

Figure 27.7: Somerset open fields: extent of detailed research, and areas where open fields are known to have been absent (after Aston 1988d, fig 5.5 and Dunning 1992; 1999) (drawing: the author)

in the north-west matching the limit of ridge and furrow and the wholly nucleated settlement very closely. There is no correlation with the different areas of heavier and lighter soils.

- To the north of Mendip evidence is rather limited but the open field systems appear to have been more irregular.
- In the lowlands west of the Parrett there were some small-scale open fields, but they were not comparable to the regular two- or three-field systems in the south-east of Somerset that embraced most of the agricultural land within a parish. What open field agriculture there was in the west of Somerset occurred in small irregular systems associated with one of several hamlets within a parish, and which covered a small proportion of the agricultural land. There were also places in this region that appear to have lacked open fields all together.
- In the far south and south-west of Somerset there is very little evidence for open field farming at all.

Farming regions

A series of historical studies have worked towards mapping patterns of landuse in the past, though as one goes further back in time sources become more fragmentary and

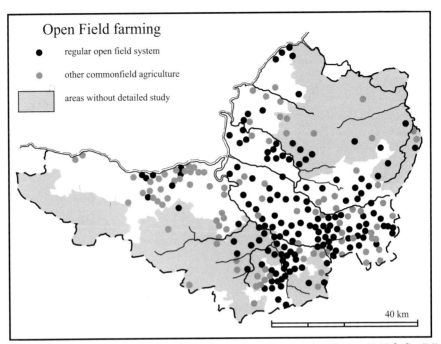

Open Field farming

● regular open field system

● other commonfield agriculture

☐ areas without detailed study

40 km

Figure 27.8: Somerset open fields: documentary evidence (after Aston 1988d, fig 5.5; Corcos 2002; Dunning 1992; 1999; Keil 1964; Musgrove 1999; Rippon 1993; 1997) (drawing: the author)

the overall picture more conjectural. The different historical sources also record different data in different ways making it impossible to give a standard description of the agricultural regimes at that time. What follows is, therefore, a generalised overview of the agriculture in Somerset over the past millennium in an attempt to see whether there is any correlation with historic landscape character.

In the Domesday Survey the uplands of Mendip, the Quantocks, and Exmoor, along with the lower-lying parts of the Somerset Levels were unoccupied; the Blackdown Hills and eastern hills were sparsely occupied (Fig 27.9). Arable cultivation was extensive elsewhere, with the greatest density of ploughteams in the lowlands west of the Parrett, parts of the south-east region, and in the north between Bath and Bristol (Fig 27.10; Darby 1967, figs 84–6; Welldon Finn and Wheatley 1967, figs 37, 39). There is a broad correlation between the density of population and plough teams in the 11th century, but no correlation with those areas whose historic landscape was characterised by nucleated villages and open fields (see below). Of the other landuses recorded, meadow was abundant in the whole of northern and eastern Somerset, while not surprisingly pasture was most abundant on and around the uplands of Mendip, the Blackdown Hills, the Quantocks, and Exmoor (Darby 1967, 91–2; Welldon Finn and Wheatley 1967, figs 42–3). Of the livestock only sheep show significant patterning, being most abundant in the north-east (Welldon Finn and Wheatley 1967, fig 49).

For the 13th/early 14th centuries, the national overview of demesne agriculture by Campbell (2000), supplemented by the more detailed studies of the manors of

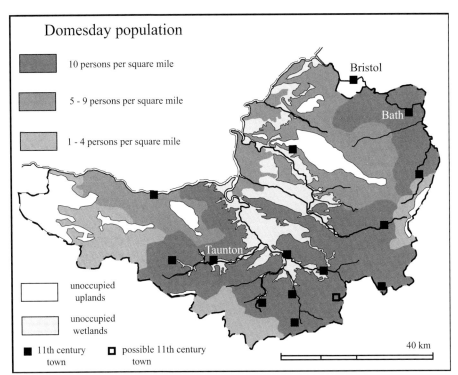

Domesday population

■ 10 persons per square mile

  5 - 9 persons per square mile

  1 - 4 persons per square mile

  unoccupied
  uplands

  unoccupied
  wetlands

■ 11th century   □ possible 11th century
  town   town

Bristol

Bath

Taunton

40 km

*Figure 27.9: Somerset: Domesday population, after Welldon Finn and Wheatley
(1967, figs 39–40) but adjusted for the fact that some areas were totally unoccupied.
11th-century towns after Aston (1986) and Hill (1982) (drawing: the author)*

Glastonbury Abbey (Keil 1964; Ecclestone 1996; Harrison 1997), and the Victoria
County Histories (Dunning 1974; 1981; 1985; 1992; 1999) allow a number of farming
zones to be identified (Fig 27.11). Mixed farming was found across most of lowland
Somerset with significant areas of arable both east and west of the Parrett. Cattle
predominated amongst the livestock in these areas (south of Mendip), notably on
manors adjacent to the Somerset Levels that also had herds of pigs. There is a strong
link here with the 'fen-edge related communities' identified in Figure 27.4; although
the wetlands in these backfens had seen relatively little reclamation they would still
have offered fertile pastures and meadow. Glastonbury's major arable manors were
located on the Polden Hills and the lowlands south (High Ham) and east (Pennard) of
Glastonbury, all in central Somerset. Its manors adjacent to the valleys flowing into
the eastern side of the Levels tended to specialise in dairying (Baltonsborough,
Butleigh, Glastonbury, and Pilton), while manors located wholly on the Levels (or
islands within them: Brent, Godney, Meare, Sowy, and Withy) specialised in dairying
and stock-raising, with the arable production including a very high proportion of
legumes (for fodder). Sheep were once again often more important around Mendip and
on the limestone hills to the north (Doulting, Houndstreet, Marksbury, Mells, and
Wrington) (and see Campbell 2000, figs 3.0–3.06, 3.14).

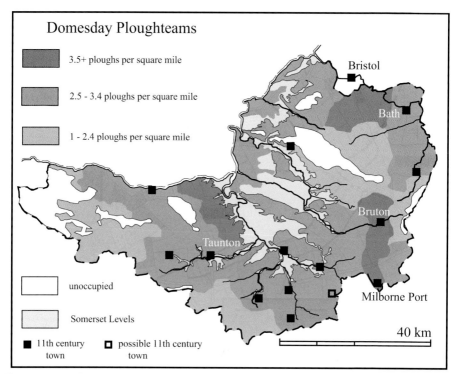

Figure 27.10: Somerset: Domesday ploughteams, after Welldon Finn and Wheatley (1967, figs 37–8) but adjusted for the fact that some areas were totally unoccupied. 11th-century towns after Aston (1986) and Hill (1982)

By the 16th/early 17th centuries Somerset was a largely pastoral county, with stock raising predominating in the west and dairying in the east (Fig 27.12; Thirsk 1967b). Communities living on the Somerset Levels and fen-edge still pursued a largely pastoral regime with an emphasis on fattening rather than dairying (ibid, 77). The main arable area was in fact the lowlands of western Somerset: in the Vales of Taunton and Wellington, for example, farmers were rearing cattle and sheep, while a few were dairymen; fruit and hops were grown alongside wheat, barley, oats, and beans (ibid 75, 79). The 'village zone' was by now a largely dairying and cloth-making region and was not self-sufficient in cereals (ibid, 79–80).

This series of snapshots of the regional agrarian economies of Somerset reveals several key conclusions: firstly, that the predominant landuse of the various regions changed significantly over time (so shaping historic landscape character), and secondly, that there is no correlation between the 'village zone' and high population, and the suitability for soils for arable farming. The 'village zone' does not represent an 'arable' or 'core' region of greatest agricultural potential within the county.

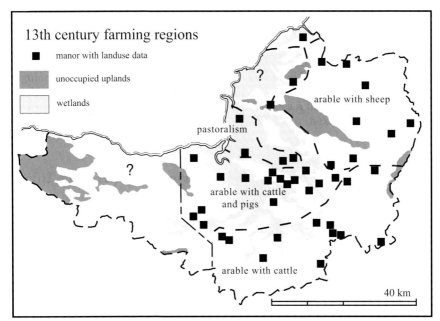

Figure 27.11: Somerset: 13th-century farming regions after Campbell (2000), Ecclestone (1996), and Keil (1964). There is no data for the west of the county (drawing: the author)

Discussion: population, economy and lordship

A detailed analysis of *why* south-east and central Somerset saw the creation of Midland-style open field/village landscapes is beyond the scope of this study, though certain observations can be made in the light of the material presented above. The date when the 'village landscape' emerged in Somerset is unclear, though evidence points to a date (or dates) between the 9th and 12th centuries being most likely. Fieldwork has shown that the village of Shapwick existed by the end of the 10th century and the context for its creation appears to have been the fragmentation of the large 'multiple/federative estate' of Pouholt, a process that place-name evidence suggests was complete by Domesday (Aston and Gerrard 1999; and see Costen 1992a; b; Rippon 1997a).

Various arguments have been put forward suggesting that villages and open fields were created in response to pressures relating to resources: over population, a scarcity of meadow/pasture, or poor drainage. In common with other areas of England, the suggestion that it was population growth that stimulated the reorganisation of rural landscapes (eg Thirsk 1964; 1966) can be dismissed (eg Williamson 2003, 28–32). There is no simple correlation with areas of high population in 11th-century Somerset and its nucleated settlements/open fields. While south-east and central Somerset did have amongst the highest densities of population in Domesday, so did a number of areas that did not have nucleated settlement/open fields. The lowlands around Taunton and Bath had amongst the highest densities of population

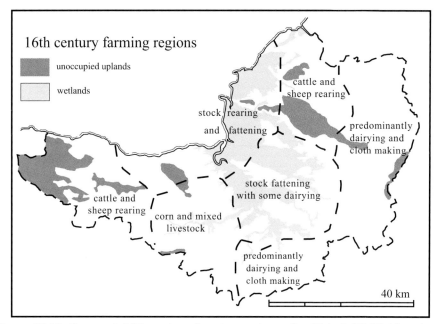

16th century farming regions

unoccupied uplands

wetlands

cattle and
sheep rearing

stock rearing
and fattening

predominantly
dairying and
cloth making

stock fattening
with some dairying

cattle and
sheep rearing

corn and mixed
livestock

predominantly
dairying and
cloth making

40 km

Figure 27.12: Somerset: 16th-century farming regions after Thirsk (1967) (drawing: the author)

and ploughteams in Domesday Somerset, and indeed the whole of south-west England, yet lay outside the 'village zone'. It has also been argued that open fields were created in response to the increasing proportion of a community's land that was being placed under arable cultivation, leading to a lack of meadow and pasture (Lewis *et al* 1997, 199). In Somerset, at least, this does not appear to have been an issue as the numerous rivers that flowed into the Somerset Levels afforded good meadowland, which is reflected in the Domesday Survey; communities in the 'village zone' of south-east and central Somerset had amongst the largest amounts of meadow in the county (Welldon Finn and Wheatley 1967, fig 42). The third resources-related factor – soils and poor drainage – has recently been promoted by Williamson (2003) who puts forward a strong case for this being a significant factor in the East Midlands. In Somerset, however, there does not appear to be a particu-larly strong link.

It does not appear, therefore, that communities were directly forced to reorganise their landscapes due to pressure from population, the increasing proportion of land under the plough, or as a response to poor drainage. In contrast, other possible expla-nations for the creation of villages and open fields suggest that it was part of wider economic circumstances. It has been observed elsewhere that the creation of nucleated villages and open fields around the 10th century occurred just as the economy showed signs of expansion, which is reflected in the emergence of new urban market centres and the more widespread production and trading of pottery (Lewis *et al* 1997, 199). The 'village zone' in Somerset, however, does not show a very strong link with that part of Somerset which had the greatest density of pre-Conquest urban

128

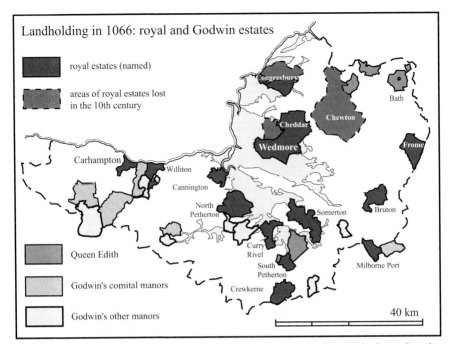

Landholding in 1066: royal and Godwin estates

royal estates (named)

areas of royal estates lost in the 10th century

Queen Edith

Godwin's comital manors

Godwin's other manors

Congresbury

Bath

Chewton

Cheddar

Wedmore

Frome

Carhampton

Williton

Cannington

North Petherton

Somerton

Bruton

Curry Rivel

South Petherton

Milborne Port

Crewkerne

40 km

Figure 27.13: Somerset landholding in 1066 – royal (labelled) and Godwin family estates (drawing: the author)

centres. These towns, particularly those with mints, may represent 'a series of new market centres, chosen by the king to fully exploit the commercial potential of his estates' (Hill 1982, 117; and see Aston 1986, fig 7.7). This suggestion that the king may have played a direct role in promoting economic development in this region raises the possibility that he may also have been responsible for reorganising the rural landscape in order to increase its productivity. The link between patterns of landholding and landscape character have long been recognised, for example in Everitt's (1985, 4) two-fold division between 'manorial' parishes where all the land was owned by a single magnate or a few large landowners, and 'freeholders' parishes where land was divided between a multiplicity of owners. The former was far more common in the 'Midland zone' of nucleated villages (eg Northamptonshire where around two-thirds of the parishes were in the hands of magnates), and the latter typical of the SouthEast and west Britain (eg Kent where just one-third of the county formed part of major estates).

In 1066, perhaps half of Somerset formed part of major estates though they were concentrated in the central part of the county. The distribution of royal and related estates in Domesday is presented here in Figure 27.13. The king held a series of ancient properties spread across Somerset including a number in the 'village zone' of central and south-east Somerset,[14] and Cheddar. Other royal estates,[15] however, lay outside the 'village zone', including those that had formerly existed at Congresbury and Chew in north Somerset (Corcos 2002; Rippon 2004). Though cumulatively extensive, these estates were, therefore, scattered across the county and show no direct link with landscapes characterised by nucleated villages and open fields.

129

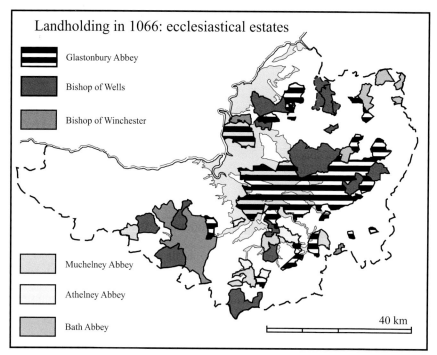

Landholding in 1066: ecclesiastical estates

Glastonbury Abbey

Bishop of Wells

Bishop of Winchester

Muchelney Abbey

Athelney Abbey

Bath Abbey

40 km

Figure 27.14: Somerset landholding in 1066 – ecclesiastical estates after Bettey 1988 (drawing: the author)

In 1066, another major landholder in Somerset was the Godwinson family, notably King Harold (Williams 1980; Fleming 1983; 1991, 59–72). These estates were acquired from a variety of means, including the illegal seizure of estates from the church,[16] grants of ancient royal demesne,[17] or were part of an ancient set of estates set aside for royal officials or as part of earldoms that were granted to members of the Godwinson family (as denoted by the payment of third-penny borough right and/or listed as *mansiones de comitatu* in the Exeter Domesday).[18] Most of these manors made payments of *albo argento* ('white silver'), as did the majority of the other Godwinson estates.[19] The payments of third-penny and white silver clearly suggest a strong link between these manors and the royal estate, while the configuration of later parish boundaries also shows that several of these Godwinson manors represent subdivisions of once larger units.[20] Taken together, whilst having a significant presence in south-east Somerset, these royal estates – both those held as the King's demesne or occasionally granted out to his Earls – were far from being the dominant landowner in the 'village zone' and so cannot have been solely responsible for reorganising all these landscapes.

There is one place in Somerset where we have a very clear idea who was responsible for village planning: Shapwick and the other manors of Glastonbury Abbey's Polden Hills estate. In 1066 Glastonbury dominated central Somerset including much of the northern part of the 'village zone'. Its estates occupied a continuous stretch of countryside from Mells in the north-east to Woolavington some 40 km to the west, which together comprised around a third of the 'village zone'. The 'multiple' or 'federative' estate based on the Polden Hills was granted to Glastonbury in the early 8th century, long before it is thought that settlement nucleation occurred elsewhere in England, and so it would appear Glastonbury Abbey has to have been responsible for the creation of the 'village landscape' in this area at least. These parishes, including Shapwick, have a particularly distinctive landscape with a series of planned villages, many with a personal-name + '-ington' place-names, and a very even distribution of resources in the Domesday Survey (Rippon 1993; 1997, 159–62; Aston and Gerrard 1999; Corcos 2002). A similarly planned landscape of nucleated villages and open fields occupied the Glastonbury manor of Sowy to the south (Musgrove 1999; 2001), suggesting that this was a common approach by Glastonbury towards the management of its estates.

If Glastonbury Abbey – or its tenants – must have been responsible for village planning on the Poldens how far were ecclesiastical landowners elsewhere doing the same? Figure 27.14 shows the distribution of church property in Domesday, and it reveals that, once again, there was no dominant landowner in the remaining part of the 'village zone'. Glastonbury held a few outlying manors, whilst the Abbeys at Athelney and Muchelney also held a small number of estates in this area. It is also notable that an extensive area of south-west Somerset – the Bishop of Winchester's estate at Taunton Deane – lay outside the main area of 'Champion' landscape. It is also striking that the core area of the 'village zone' in south-east Somerset was not part of any royal or ecclesiastical estate. Rather, this was a landscape of fragmented lordship with a multiplicity of thanes, many of which were not even named in Domesday. It may be that there were once large estates in this area of which no evidence now survives; it may have been in the context of the fragmentation of these estates, and the creation of the thane's holdings, that landscape reorganisation occurred. More research is required on the social context of regional variation in landscape character.

The discussion so far has focused on the potential role of major landholders, but Lewis *et al.* (1997, 199–201) have argued that it was the rural communities themselves that were responsible for the replanning through an 'evolutionary process' whereby communities in regions with a bias towards arable cultivation reorganised themselves in order to adapt to the new economic circumstances, with others then emulating their neighbours. The Somerset evidence suggests that a similar 'evolutionary process' may have occurred there too, perhaps following the lead of Glastonbury Abbey. In terms of its natural environment, resources such as good meadow and pasture, Domesday population, and pattern of landholding (excepting the dominant position of Glastonbury), there seems little reason why nucleation should have been restricted to south-east and central Somerset. The existence of so many emerging urban centres certainly suggests that this was a region with a growing economy, while Glastonbury may just have provided the inspiration for others in restructuring their settlement patterns and field systems. Like ripples on a pond, the trend towards nucleation may have spread out from this core region, barely reaching the extremities of the county which show just limited signs of nucleation and small-scale irregular open field systems. Do these hybrid landscapes represent the very diluted effects of 'villagisation' on what was before a landscape of wholly dispersed settlement and enclosed fields, or in fact were these areas untouched by the *c* 10th-century replanning and represent the landscape that was swept away in central and south-east Somerset? Perhaps more detailed historic landscape characterisation could help answer that crucial question.

CASE STUDY: MEARE, SOMERSET: LINKING MAPS AND DOCUMENTS

Key features:
- *parish-scale, past-oriented historic landscape analysis used in the context of research*
- *demonstrates a clear relationship between natural and cultural landscapes*
- *integration of a wide range of sources using the historic landscape as a means of relating documentary information on the medieval agrarian landscape to physical evidence on the ground*
- *detailed research used to understand the physical processes behind the evolution of a historic landscape, and to reconstruct what that landscape looked like at particular periods in time*
- *further reading:* Musgrave 1999; Rippon in press.

Introduction

The case studies of Cornwall, Lancashire and Somerset all assessed historic landscape character over very large areas with the result that the 'types' are very generalised and cover what at a local level are quite varied landscapes. This final case study goes to the opposite end of the scale with regards to the size of case study areas that can be subject to historic landscape analysis – the parish – in order to demonstrate the degree of detail that can be achieved.

The Somerset case study shows how Glastonbury Abbey was the dominant land-owner in medieval Somerset, and this is an examination of the origins and development of the historic landscape in the one of its manors: Meare, in the Somerset Levels. The surviving archives of Glastonbury Abbey contain a wealth of material relating to socio-economic and agrarian history and have seen a series of seminal studies on the management of a medieval estate (eg Postan 1952/3; 1955/6; 1975; Lennard 1955/6; 1975; Holt 1987; Carley 1988; Abrams and Carley 1991) and been the subject of a number of theses (Keil 1964; Stacey 1972; Ecclestone 1996; Harrison 1997; Musgrove 1999; Thompson 1997; Corcos 2002). Very little work has, however, been carried out on reconstructing what the medieval landscape of the individual manors actually looked like, and how they changed over time. The following case study shows how historic landscape analysis can be used to achieve just this.

The historic landscape types

Meare is a bedrock island in the Brue Valley, part of the Somerset Levels immediately west of Glastonbury. Immediately to the south of the island, and to the west/north of a

---

Figure 28.1.A: Meare, Somerset: the landscape in 1806 (drawing: the author).
B: Meare, Somerset: major landscape elements, including settlements, selected major artificial watercourses, and reconstructed droveways (drawing: the author)

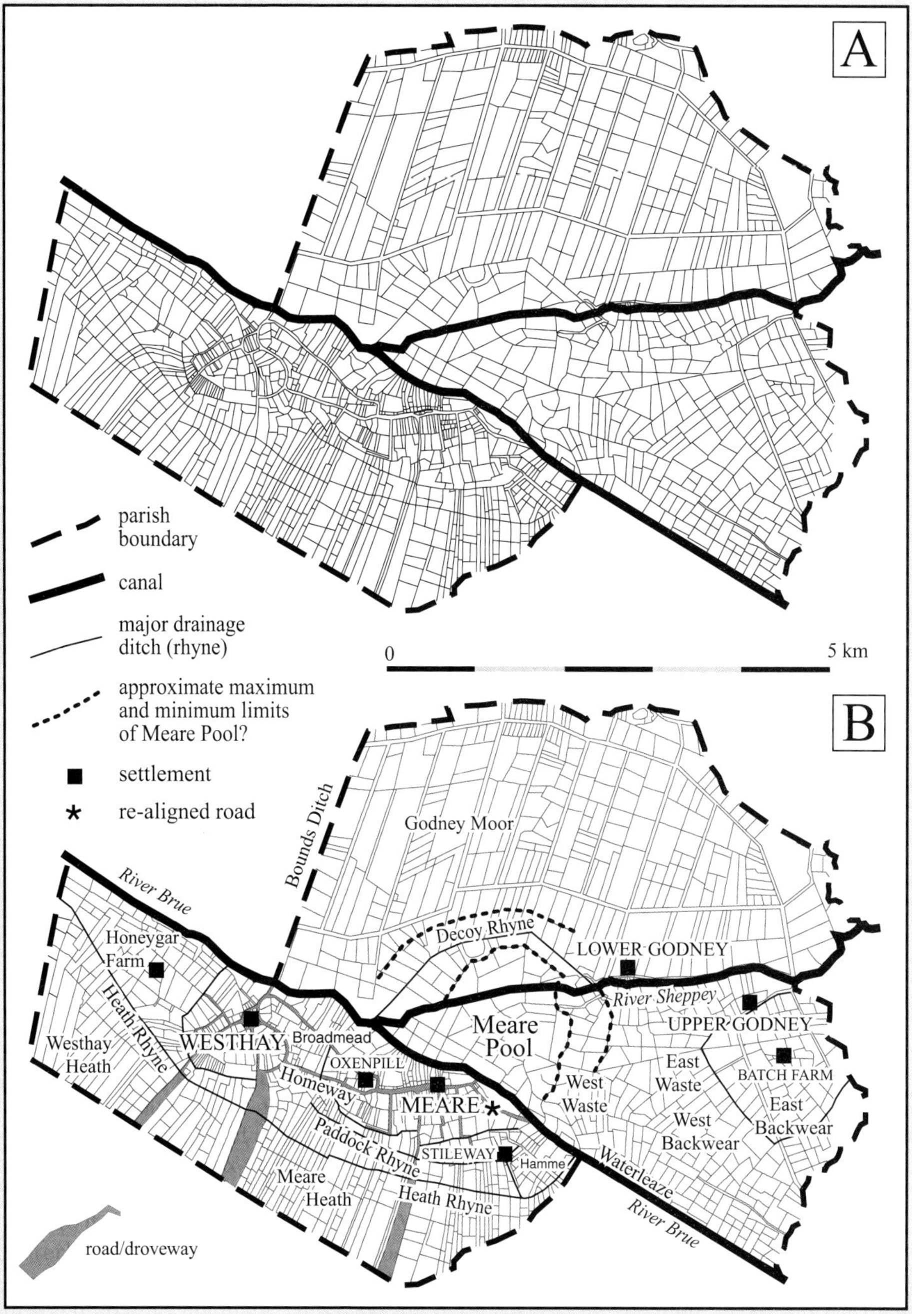
A
B
parish boundary
canal
major drainage ditch (rhyne)
approximate maximum and minimum limits of Meare Pool?
settlement
re-aligned road
0
5 km
road/droveway
Godney Moor
Bounds Ditch
River Brue
Honeygar Farm
Heath Rhyne
Westhay Heath
WESTHAY
Broadmead
OXENPILL
Homeway
MEARE
Paddock Rhyne
STILEWAY
Hamme
Meare Heath
Heath Rhyne
Decoy Rhyne
LOWER GODNEY
River Sheppey
UPPER GODNEY
Meare Pool
West Waste
East Waste
BATCH FARM
West Backwear
East Backwear
Waterleaze
River Brue

large former lake (Meare Pool), there are peat bogs while to the east there are extensive areas of alluvial soil. Figure 28.1.A shows Meare parish in 1806 (the earliest date for which we have a complete map). A number of key features in the landscape can be identified, such as major drainage ditches and fen banks around which field systems were subsequently planned (Fig 28.1.B: Paddock Rhyne, Heath Rhyne; 'rhyne' is the local word for an artificial watercourse which in these cases would have run alongside the fen bank). The historic landscape as a whole can be broken down into a series of generic landscape 'types' that occur in one or more unique 'character areas' (Fig 28.2 and Table 4).

Understanding the processes of landscape formation

As described in Part Two, different landscape morphologies give an indication of the processes that led to their formation and subsequent use, and this becomes clearer through documentary analysis (Table 5; Musgrove 1999). The highly rectilinear patterns of roads and fields on Godney and Westhay Moors, for example, were created in 1783 when the area was enclosed (SRO Q/Rde 125). The pattern of fields around the eastern fringes of Westhay (the 'short strips' type) are suggestive of enclosed former common meadows, and the Tithe Map field-names support this (eg Broadmead: SRO D/D/Rt 423; Broadmead can in fact be traced back to a survey of Meare carried out for Abbott Monnington in 1355 when it was indeed meadow: Musgrove 1999, 276). The regular (longitudinal) field type is interesting in that it appears to have been created in a number of stages. Initially a series of narrow fields were laid out from the fen-edge as far as Paddock Rhyne, and then extended, sometimes with a change in orientation, to Heath Rhyne, and finally as far as the parish boundary (Fig 28.1.B). The manorial account rolls for Meare suggest that the first stage was already completed by 1343/4, describing Meare and Westhay Heaths as 'waste' to the 'south of *Hamweye*' [Hammes], 'outside the south part of *Henangre*' [Honeygar], and 'outside the south part of *Halperryparroke*' [Paddock Rhyne??].

The area of 'irregular, large' fields north of Meare Island can be identified as the former Meare Pool that was drained and enclosed in the 17th century. A survey of the manor of Meare carried out for Abbot Beere in 1515 described Meare Pool as being one mile long and three-quarters of a mile wide, while another survey conducted at the time of the Dissolution of the Monasteries in 1539 described it as 'circuit five miles, and one mile and an half broad' (Phelps 1836). The first serious attempt at its drainage was in the early 17th century, as in 1630 Mr William Freake is described as having drained many hundreds of acres there; in 1638 there is reference to 480 acres of ground 'lately a fish pool' (Williams 1970, 106), and in 1641, tithes ceased to be paid on fishing, swans, fuel, and turves in *le Mere* as 'the water was drained away' (Harris 1991, 87). In 1684 an enquiry into the tithes owed from the newly reclaimed land stated that 'New Cutts' (Decoy Rhyne: Fig 28.1.B) was dug some 25 years earlier (ie *c 1660) so creating the historic landscape of today (Williams 1970, 106).*

134

TABLE 4: *Historic landscape character types in Meare, Somerset*

Field boundary pattern	Roads	Settlement	Soils	Character areas	Interpretation
Irregular, large: *large fields of irregular, largely polygonal, layout with little or no sign of overall planning. Incorporate the meandering lines of former natural streams.*	absent	absent	alluvium	?Meare Pool	enclosure of last part of Meare Pool to be drained; 17th century
Irregular, small: *small fields of irregular, rectangular, or polygonal shape with little or no sign of overall planning.*	sinuous, with areas of roadside 'waste'	mostly spread along roads	dryland	?Meare Island ?Westhay Island	piecemeal enclosure; mostly medieval
Sinuous coaxial: *blocks of rectangular and long-narrow fields laid out between curving/sinuous axial boundaries*	sinuous, with areas of roadside 'waste'	restricted to road	dryland	?Meare Island	enclosure of former open field furlongs (laid out *c 10th–12th century?); late medieval* to 19th century
Tenement plots: *series of long narrow plots with sub-division at street frontage containing buildings.*	sinuous, with areas of roadside 'waste'	in 'toft'-like plots along road	dryland	?Meare Island ??Westhay Island	planned village tenements; *c* 10th–12th century?

TABLE 4 (contd)

Field boundary pattern	Roads	Settlement	Soils	Character areas	Interpretation
Short strips: *short, narrow, straight-sided fields laid out in small discrete blocks*	absent	absent	fen-edge and alluvial margins	?around Westhay Island	enclosed meadow; medieval. Pattern of long narrow fields suggest a former common meadow
Intermediate: largely rectangular fields, with some indication of rudimentary structure, but no evidence for overall planning.					
sub-types (Fig 28.2) blocks of rectangular fields, varying in shape from square to long/narrow	mostly straight, with little roadside 'waste'	occasional isolated farm	Alluvium and fen-peat	?East Backwear ?East &West Waste, and W Backwear ?Honeygar	areas of reclamation; late medieval/early post medieval. Pattern of fields suggest a landscape held in severalty
blocks of small rectangular fields	absent	absent	Alluvium, fen peat and raised bog	?The Hammes	A discrete medieval reclamation. Pattern of long-narrow fields suggest a former common meadow
Regular (rectilinear): planned landscape structured around long, parallel longitudinal roads and rhynes that create a series of 'blocks'	straight, forming axial elements of the landscape	absent	raised bog and fen peat	?Godney & Westhay Moors	18th-century reclamation

TABLE 4 (contd)

Field boundary pattern	Roads	Settlement	Soils	Character areas	Interpretation
sub-types (Fig 28.2)	A 'blocks' undivided creating predominantly rectangular fields				
	B 'blocks' sub-divided further into long, narrow fields				
	C mostly rectilinear (occasionally polygonal) fields between outer major axial element of landscape and edge of enclosed area				
Regular (longitudinal): planned blocks with a dominant longitudinal axis creating long, narrow fields, all of same orientation, structured around long, parallel longitudinal droveways and rhynes.	broad, funnel shaped droveways forming axial elements of the landscape (highlighted on Fig 30.2).	absent	raised bog peat	?Meare & Westhay Heaths	Early post-medieval reclamation. Changes of direction at lateral rhynes suggest episodic expansion.
sub-types (see Figure 28.2)	1 long, relatively broad, blocks with very few lateral sub-divisions				
	2 long, relatively broad blocks with lateral sub-divisions				
	3 long, relatively broad blocks with lateral and some short longitudinal subdivisions				
	4 long, narrow fields with very few lateral sub-divisions				
	5 long, narrow fields with lateral sub-divisions				
Infill: small plots filling the space between major landscape features/other character areas	various	various	often fen-edge and wetland margins	?various locations	areas of reclamation and enclosure; various dates

The historic landscape character areas

Once the processes that lay behind the creation of the different historic landscape types have been established, and their character described, a series of unique character areas emerge that correspond to the phases of reclamation (Table 5). This leads on to Figure 28.3 which shows reconstructions of what this landscape may have looked like in *c* 1300 and *c* 1500. The first of these dates relates to a period when the landscape of Meare is particularly well documented, notably with the survey carried

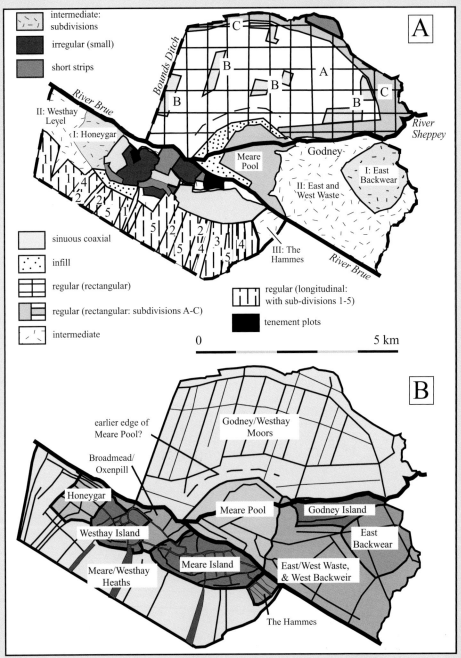

Figure 28.2: A: Meare, Somerset: historic landscape types (drawing: the author).
B: Meare, Somerset: historic landscape areas (drawing: the author)

138

TABLE 5: Historic landscape character areas in Meare, Somerset

Character area	Landscape type(s)	soils
Meare Island	irregular, intermediate, sinuous coaxial, short strips and tenement plots	dryland and adjacent fen-edge

Complex landscape comprising a manor complex within a walled precinct, adjacent church and planned village, open fields (sinuous coaxial type landscape), and some fen-edge reclamation (all documented). Three modern settlement foci of which Meare village appears to comprise a discrete block of planned tenements, whereas Oxenpill consists of a looser agglomeration of farmsteads and cottages. In its present form Stileway is 19th-century, though 'building land' is referred to there in 1340.

Westhay Island	irregular, intermediate, short strips and (?) tenement plots	dryland and adjacent fen-edge

Complex landscape, with a possible small block of planned tenements to south-west of Manor House Farm. Irregular fields on dryland, with area of fen-edge enclosures/ reclamation (short-strip type landscape) to south and west. No 'sinuous coaxial' type landscape suggestive of former open fields.

Godney Island	irregular	dryland, fen-edge and adjacent alluvium

Area of mostly irregular fields on and around the bedrock island (though only really evident on the ground, not the 1806 map). A long sinuous boundary runs west from Godney Farm along the watershed of the bedrock ridge. The modern hamlet (Lower Godney) lies on the alluvium next to the Sheppey, though historically the settlement focus may have lain on the bedrock/fen-edge at Upper Godney.

Meare Pool	intermediate, and infill	alluvium

Area of irregular fields in the central/eastern area of the former Meare Pool, which postdate the canalized River Sheppey (now the James Weir River). Defined on the north/west by a sinuous boundary that may represent an earlier limit to its drainage/enclosure; the area between this boundary and Decoy Rhyne is one field wide and of 'infill' type landscape: Fig 28.1). Intermittent field boundary to the north/west of, and concentric with, Decoy Pool Rhyne and limit of flooding on 16th January 1947 (shown on air photographs), might suggest the original maximum limit of the Pool. The drainage and enclosure of Meare Pool started in the early 17th century (see above).

East Backwear	intermediate	alluvium

Area of intermediate fields,centred on Batch Farm, little different in character to areas to the west and south, but bounded by a near continuous rhyne defining a sub-rectangular enclosure. In 1515 Estbackweare is described as arable in the West Field of Godney.

East & West Waste, and West Backwear	intermediate	alluvium, fen peat

Area of intermediate fields showing greater regularity in the east (West Backwear) than the west (East and West Waste, and Waterleaze). The first mention of Waterleas (Waterleaze) was in 1515 when it was described as pasture. The phrase 'The bounds of Bacchyngwere' is referred to in 1351 though it is unclear whether any reclamation had occurred. In 1515 Westbackweare and Estbackweare (West and East Backwear to the south of Godney Hill) are described as arable in the West Field of Godney, which implies that quite a sizeable chunk of moor had been reclaimed.

TABLE 5 (contd)

Character area	Landscape type(s)	soils
Broadmead and Oxenpill	intermediate	alluvium

Area of irregular (Splotts) and intermediate (Broadmead and Westmead) landscape on the dryland between Meare and Westhay spreading onto the alluvium to the north, representing reclamation rooted on the fen-edge. Homeway Road (between Meare and Westhay) cuts through these fields. *Brodemede* (Broadmead) and *Oxenpull* (modern Oxenpill) are first mentioned in 1355.

The Hammes (SE of Stileway)	intermediate	alluvium

Area of intermediate landscape on the alluvium east of Meare island, representing a discrete reclamation: the long, narrow fields may suggest that it was once a common meadow, or simply the medieval tradition of creating long narrow fields which in a wetland have the advantage of a relatively long length of drainage ditch per area enclosed. Documented in 1260 as *Hammesmede*.

Honeygar (Westhay Level)	intermediate	alluvium

Area of rectangular fields formed by a series of long axial boundaries parallel with the Brue. Williams (1970, fig 12) shows this area as having been reclaimed *c* 1400–1600 (though no evidence is given), but meadow and pasture at a place called *Henangre* or *Henacre* is documented from 1301/2, presumably Hennigans (now Honeygar Farm). The frequency of references to Hennigans in early 14th-century sources suggest that clarification of rights and dues was needed, perhaps because of active reclamation in the area between the islands of Westhay and Burtle. The field systems in the southern part of this area predate Heath Rhyne.

Meare and Westhay Heaths	regular (longitudinal) with a series of variants	raised bog peat

Extensive planned landscape based upon closely-spaced axial boundaries and long, narrow fields. These boundaries appear to have run initially between the fen-edge and Paddock Rhyne, then Heath Rhyne (as far as Honeygar), and were finally extended, sometimes with a slight change of direction (most obviously to the SW of Westhay and SE of Meare), from Heath Rhyne to the parish boundary. Some of these long narrow fields were not enclosed further, while others were subdivided both laterally and longitudinally (Fig 30.2). References to meadow on the south side of Meare Island in 1355 (at Allen's Moor, Stileway, *Southeth*, and *Hethmor*) may represent the first stage of this reclamation). The Account Roll for 1343/4 describes 'waste' at *Hethmor* 'south of *Hamweye*' [Hammes], 'outside the south part of *Henangre*' [Honeygar], and 'outside the south part of *Halperryparroke*' [Paddock Rhyne?].

Godney and Westhay Moors	regular (rectilinear) with three variants	raised bog and fen peat

Extensive planned landscape based on a series of roughly north-south oriented roads and rhynes, and two roughly east-west oriented roads laid out concentric with the northern parish boundary. The blocks they define are subdivided into a wide variety of rectangular fields, some of which are further subdivided into long, narrow plots; there is a less regular layout where the area between the outer-most axial roads and the parish boundary was enclosed. Enclosed 1783.

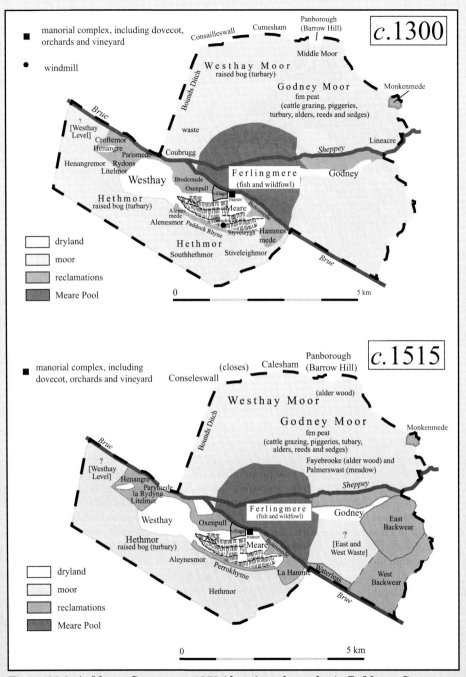

Figure 28.3: A: Meare, Somerset, c 1350 (drawing: the author). B: Meare, Somerset, c 1500 (drawing: the author)

out by Abbot Ford in 1260, and a run of account rolls (1257–1344); the latter date corresponds to the Survey of Abbot Beere in 1515.

Initially reclamation focused on the alluvial marshes to the west, north and east of the bedrock island. The field-names (mostly being '-ha and '-mead'), surviving medieval surveys and account rolls suggest the marshes were mostly used for meadow (providing winter fodder for livestock). The peat moors were left as unenclosed pasture rich in wetland resources, which the manorial surveys, court rolls, and legal records of a series of disputes suggest included the rights of turbary (peat cutting for fuel), sedges and reeds (for thatch and animal bedding), and most importantly grazing for cattle and pigs, and alder woodland. 'Ferlingmere' (Meare Pool) was the abbey's most important fishery and was also used for wildfowling. Field boundary morphology (long, narrow, strip-like fields) and documentary references suggest the meadows were mostly subdivided, and most of the arable in Meare was also arranged in an open field system which survived in part into the 19th century. The enclosure of these open fields was by agreement and the furlong boundaries retained in the post-enclosure field boundary pattern (cf Figs 28.1.A, 28.2.A and 28.3). The structure of the landscape on Westhay is unclear and requires further research.

By the early 16th century the landscape had changed little. Some former meadows had been abandoned (eg Broadmead to the north east of Westhay), though to the east of Meare and south of the island at Godney there was extensive reclamation. The field morphology here, with relatively large rectilinear fields is suggestive of enclosures held in severalty and not common/open fields.

This case study illustrates another simple example of landscape evolution, showing how information contained within the historic countryside itself can be integrated with documentary sources to both recreate what the landscape looked like at a particular point in time, and how it changed over time. Past patterns of landuse, and something of the social/tenurial structure within which it occurred, can also be reconstructed. Meare is just one of over 50 manors held by Glastonbury and the scope for reconstructing and understanding the medieval landscape on such well-documented estates is enormous.

PART FOUR
TOWARDS A MODEL OF GOOD PRACTICE

The historic character of the countryside has been created through the interaction of human societies and their environment, most notably through various forms of subsistence, communication, recreation, and defence. Historic landscape analysis is based upon an objective understanding of the cultural processes that have given the rural environment its current appearance. Unlike the traditional material studied by archaeologists (buried and relict features/sites/landscapes), the countryside is a complete historical document in its own right (though the survival of features from any particular period may be fragmentary due to a constant evolution). It comprises a set of physical cultural features (eg elements such as its field boundaries that together form parcels such as fields, and landscape components such as field systems) draped across the natural environment. These individual elements interact with each other (eg elements of a settlement pattern are linked by roads which pass through field systems), and it is this articulation of different landscape components in both time and space that leads to different historic landscape character. While currently used mostly for rural areas, the principles of historic landscape characterisation are equally applicable to understanding the origins, development, and cultural associations of urban landscapes as work in Cornwall and Lancashire is starting to show.

Today, most landscapes are palimpsests, comprising a range of elements that combine in a particular way to give rise to a certain character. In some cases landscapes were subject to an 'event', notably a replanning, which led to the creation of an enduring pattern, but in such cases it must not be forgotten that there has been a history of subsequent evolution that will have to a greater or lesser degree changed that original 'design'. Other landscapes will simply have evolved gradually over time and as such their complex nature will be reflected in their historic character. It is important not to lose sight of the fact that the historic landscape was constructed and used by people, whether they were acting as individuals, institutions or communities, and for many areas we have an abundance of documentary material for the different patterns of lordship and community. If we are to understand how different historic landscape characters came about, then we must explore the potential role that these social factors played.

There is no single methodology for historic landscape analysis; just as historic landscape character varies so dramatically, so do the reasons for studying it. The output of historic landscape analysis can be considered as a 'past-oriented' understanding of the origins and development of that landscape, and a 'future-oriented' description of historic landscape character to inform planners and countryside managers. The aim of this handbook has been to introduce some of these many different approaches that have been used to date so that the reader can pick and mix elements to suit their own research agenda. There are, however, some underlying elements of good practice that can be suggested. Before embarking upon historic landscape analysis, consideration should be given to a number of factors that will effect the size of the study area that can be tackled, or the level of detail that can be achieved if the study area is predetermined:

- Extent: how large is the study area?
- Complexity: how diverse and complex is the historic landscape within the study area?
- Sources of data: are the necessary base-maps available? what other datasets are available (eg existing mapping of relict features/landscapes from air photography)?
- Knowledge/expertise: what previous research has been carried out on this or analogous landscapes?
- Requirements of known and likely users: planners, countryside managers, local and regional historians and archaeologists

KEY POINTS

- Mapping must occur against a backdrop showing individual fields; 1:25,000 is generally found to be the most appropriate for large-scale work (eg county-scale) since this balances the requirement for field-scale data with a broad overview of the landscape, and the need to avoid getting bogged down with too much detail. For smaller-scale work, 1:10,000/First Edition Six Inch maps will give greater precision on the size/shape of fields, and individual relationships between field boundaries.

- If the primary aim is to understand the origins and development of the landscape, the earliest complete cartographic sources should be used. Although for many areas these are the Tithe Maps of *c* 1840 these only cover individual parishes and are large and cumbersome to use. It is generally easier to use the First Edition Six Inch maps of *c* 1880, transcribing any changes shown on the Tithe Maps (ie deleting boundaries on the Six Inch maps that postdate the Tithe Survey etc).

- If the primary aim is to advise planners and countryside managers then a case can be made for using modern maps as the backdrop for HLC, though the earliest possible cartographic sources must still be consulted in order to gain the best possible understanding of the historic character of a particular area.

- Relict (ie no longer functioning) features can form part of the character of historic landscapes. Such features may be earlier unrelated relict landscapes (eg areas of ridge and furrow underlying a field system created through Parliamentary Enclosure), or may simply be elements of the historic landscape that have gone out of use (eg abandoned field boundaries or deserted settlement). Such relict landscapes and features can be vital in understanding the origins and development of historic landscape character.

- The historic landscape can be broken down into a series of interlinked components (or themes), notably field systems, settlement, and communications. For research purposes other layers might include place- and field-names, landownership in the Tithe Survey, and relict landscapes or features. The most powerful way of managing and manipulating this data is to use a GIS, though if this is not practical then each dataset can be produced to the same scale (ie 1:25,000 etc) on sheets of tracing paper or permatrace.

144

- An area of historic landscape can also be broken down into a series of generic 'historic landscape types', which are not area-specific (and which can be further simplified into a series of still generic 'zones'). In specific places, the particular combination of landscape features, types, and zones combine to form distinct 'character areas'.

- Historic landscape analysis is at its most powerful when used as a means of integrating a wide range of source material, including cartographic and documentary material, place- and field-names, and archaeological evidence from buried or relict components of both the historic landscape and what it replaced.

Notes

1. Essex Records Office D/CT 154.
2. Essex Records Office TS/M 63/9.
3. Essex Records Office D/DMq E7/1.
4. Essex Records Office D/DQs 28.
5. Huntingdon Records Office 1716/54.
6. 'Broom Wood' is the earliest name for this area (1777: Chapman and Andre); following 19th century woodland regeneration it was known as 'Coxall Wood' (1867: First Edition OS Six Inch map) and Solbys Wood (1923: Third Edition OS Six Inch map). There is no known historical name for the area of late 18th century woodland clearance to the west, though on the Tithe Survey it was divided between field number 145–6 and 148–8.
7. The clearest evidence for this is shown on the Tithe Map to the north of Sayers Farm; by the First Edition OS Six Inch map these boundaries had been straightened, reminding us of the need to consult the earliest available cartographic sources.
8. Great Wood and West Wood were held by the Dean and Chapter of St Paul's Cathedral, London; Horseleigh Wood was held by Prittlewell Priory, Essex, and later St Paul's; Pound Wood was the property of Westminster Abbey, London (Rackham 1986, 17, 21, 88; Rippon 1999a).
9. Solbys, Bramble Hall and Garold's Farms (Reaney 1935, 185; Yearsley 1998, 30).

10. The Peak District Natinal Park and then the rest of Derbyshire: Barnatt 1999; the now abolished county of Avon: Sydes 1999; and the Isle of Axholme in the Countryside Commission's 'Historic Landscape Character Area' of the Humberhead Levels: Miller 1999.
11. Hampshire (see Fig 15): Lambrick 1999; Tartaglia-Kershaw 1999; Fairclough *et al* 2002; the Cotswolds 'Area of Outstanding Beauty' and then the rest of Gloucestershire: Wills 1999; Nottinghamshire: Bishop 1999; Kent; and Suffolk.
12. Lancashire (see Part Three), Somerset, Herefordshire, Surrey, Hertfordshire and Essex.
13. Buckinghamshire, Cheshire, Cumbria, Devon, Dorset, the Isle of Wight, Northamptonshire, and Shropshire.

14. Bruton, Milborne Port, Crewkerne, South Petherton, Somerton (with Ilchester), Curry Rivel (with Langport).
15. Cannington, North Petherton, Carhampton, and Williton.
16. Banwell and Congresbury.
17. Crewkerne with Easthams.
18. Bath, Brompton [Regis], Henstridge, Old Cleeve, Milverton, and Winsford.
19. [Queen] Camel, Capton, Coker, Creech [St Michael], Dulverton with Brushford, Hardington [Mandiville], Nettlecombe, and North Curry; only Langford [Budville] did not make this payment.
20. eg Winsford appears to have been carved out of Dulverton; Nettlecombe from Old Cleeve.

BIBLIOGRAPHY

Aberg, A 1978 *Medieval Moated Sites*. London: CBA Res Rep **17**.

Abrams, L and Carley, J P (eds) 1991 *The Archaeology and History of Glastonbury Abbey*. Woodbridge: Boydell Press.

Aldred, O 2001 *Somerset and Exmoor National Park Historic Landscape Characterisation Project 1999–2000*. Taunton: Somerset County Council. and English Heritage.

Aldred, O 2002 Somerset and Exmoor National Park Historic Landscape Characterisation Project. *Soc for Landscape Studies Newsletter Autumn/Winter 2002*, 3–5.

Aldred, O and Fairclough, G 2003 *Historic Landscape Characterisation: Taking Stock of the Method (The English Heritage National HLC Method Review 2002)*. London: English Heritage & Somerset County Council.

Allen, J R L 1988 Reclamation and Sea Defence in Rumney Parish, Monmouthshire, *Archaeol Cambrensis* **CXXXVII**, 135–40.

Allen, J R L 2002 Retreat rates of soft-sediment cliffs: the contribution from dated fishweirs and traps on Holocene coastal outcrops, *Proc Geologists Ass* **113**, 1–8.

Aston, M 1985 *Interpreting the Landscape*. London: Batsford.

Aston, M 1986 Post Roman Central Places in Somerset, in Grant, E (ed.) *Central Places, Archaeology and History*. Sheffield: Univ Sheffield Dept of Archaeology, 49–78.

Aston. M 1988a *Medieval Fish, Fisheries and Fishponds in England*. Oxford: BAR Brit. Ser. **182**.

Aston, M 1988b *Aspects of the Medieval Landscape of Somerset*. Taunton: Somerset County Council.

Aston, M 1988c Settlement Patterns and Form, in Aston, M (ed.) 1988b, 67–82.

Aston, M 1988d Landuse and fields systems, in Aston, M (ed.) 1988b, 83–8.

Aston, M, Costen, M D, Hall, T and Ecclestone, M 1998 The Medieval Furlongs of Shapwick: attempts at mapping the 1515 survey, in Aston, M A, Hall, T A and Gerrard, C M (eds) *The Shapwick Project: an archaeological, historical and topographical study. The Eighth Report*. Bristol, Univ Bristol Dept for Continuing Education, 104–68.

Aston, M and Gerrard, C 1999 'Unique, Traditional and Charming'. The Shapwick Project, Somerset. *Antiq J* **79**,1–58.

Aston, M and Leech, R 1977 *Historic Towns in Somerset: Archaeology and Planning*. Bristol: Comm for Rescue Archaeol in Avon, Gloucestershire and Somerset.

Aston, M and Rowley T 1974 *Landscape Archaeology*. Newton Abbot: David and Charles.

Aubrey, J. 1685 *Memoires of Natural Remarques in the County of Wiltshire*, reprinted in Ponting, K G (ed.) *Aubreys Natural History of Wiltshire*. Newton Abbott: David and Charles.

Austin, D. and Walker, M.J.C. 1985 A New Landscape Context for Hound Tor, *Med. Archaeol.* **29**, 147–52.

Baker, R A H 1965 Field patterns in seventeenth century Kent, *Geography* **50**, 18–30.

Baker, A R H 1973 Changes in the Later Middle Ages, in Darby, H C (ed.), 186–247.

Baker, A R H and Butlin, R A 1973 *Studies in British Field Systems*. Cambridge: Cambridge Univ Press.

Barnatt, J 1999 Peak National Park: A changing landscape, in Fairclough, G (ed.) 1999a, 41–50.

Bassett, S 1997 Continuity and fission in the Anglo-Saxon landscape: the origins of the Rodings (Essex), *Landscape Hist* **19**, 25–42.

Bath and North East Somerset Council 2003 *Rural Landscapes of Bath and North East Somerset: A Landscape Character Assessment*. Bath.

Bell, M, Caseldine, A and Neumann, H 2000 *Prehistoric Intertidal Archaeoloogy in the Welsh Severn Estuary*. York: CBA Res Rep 120.

Beresford, M 1954 *The Lost Villages of England*. London: Lutterworth Press.

Beresford, M W 1964 Dispersed and Grouped Settlement in Medieval Cornwall, *Agric Hist Rev* **12(i)**, 13–27.

Beresford, M and Hurst, J 1971 *Deserted Medieval Villages*. London: Lutterworth Pres.

Bettey, J 1988 The Church and the Landscape, Part 2: From the Norman Conquest to the Reformation, in Aston, M (ed.) *The Medieval Landscape of Somerset*. Taunton: Somerset County Council, 54–65.

Billingsley, J 1798 *A general View of the Agriculture of the County of Somerset*. London: C Dilly.

Bishop, M 1999 Relating research to practice in Nottinghamshire, in Fairclough, G (ed.) 1999a, 83–91.

Black, E 1987 *The Roman Villas of South-East England*. Oxford: BAR Brit Ser **171**.

Blair, J 1994 *Anglo-Saxon Oxfordshire*. Stroud: Alan Sutton.

Bloemers, J H F 2002 Past- and future-oriented archaeology: protecting and developing the archaeological-historical landscape in the Netherlands, in Fairclough, G and Rippon, S (eds) *Europe's Cultural Landscape: archaeologists and the management of change*. Brussels: Europae Archaeologiae Consilium, 89–96.

Bond, J 1988 Monastic Fisheries, in M. Aston (ed.) *Medieval Fish, Fisheries and Fishponds in England*. Oxford, BAR Brit Ser **182**, 69–112.

Bond, C J 1989 water Management in the Rural Monastery, in Gilchrist, R and Mytum, H (eds) *The Archaeology of Rural Monasteries*. Oxford: BAR Brit Ser **203**, 83–111.

Bond, J 2001 Monastic water management in Great Britain: a review, in Keevill, G, Aston, M and Hall, T (eds) *Monastic Archaeology*. Oxford: Oxbow, 88–136.

Bradley, R, Entwistle, R, and Raymond, F 1994 *Prehistoric Land Divisions on Salisbury Plain*. London: English Heritage.

Braudel, F 1988 *The Identity of France, Volume 1: History and Environment,* from the French by Sian Reynolds. London: Collins

Brown, T and Foard, G 1998 The Saxon landscape: a regional perspective. In Everson, P and Williamson, T (eds) *The Archaeology of Landscape: studies presented to Christopher Taylor*. Manchester: Manchester Univ Press, 67–94.

Brunskill, R W 1992 *Traditional Buildings of Britain*. London: Victor Gollancz.

Butlin, R A 1964 Northumberland Field Systems, *Agric Hist Rev* **XII**, 99–120.

Cadw 1998 *Register of Landscapes of Outstanding Historic Interest in Wales*. Cardiff: Cadw Welsh Historic Monuments.

Cadw 2001 *Register of Landscapes of Special Historic Interest in Wales*. Cardiff: Cadw Welsh Historic Monuments.

Campbell, B M S 2000 *English Seigniorial Agriculture, 1250–1450*. Cambridge: Cambridge Univ Press.

Campbell, B M S *et al.* 1993 *A Medieval Capital and its Grain Supply: agrarian production and distribution in the London region c.1300*. London: Inst of British Geographers.

Campbell, C, Tipping, R and Cowley, D 2002 Continuity and stability in past upland land uses in the western Cheviot Hills, southern Scotland, *Landscape History* 24, 111—18.

Carley, J 1988 *Glastonbury Abbey*. London: Guild Publishing.

Coles, B and Coles, J 1986 *Sweet Track to Glastonbury*. London: Thames and Hudson.

Coney, A. 1992 Fish, fowl and fen: landscape and economy on seventeenth-century Martin Mere, *Landscape Hist* 14, 51–64.

Coones, P 1985 One landscape or many? A geographical perspective. *Landscape Hist* **7**, 5–12.

Corcos, N 2002 *The affinities and antecedents of medieval settlement: topographical perspectives from three Somerset hundreds*. PhD, Univ of Bristol.

Corney, M 2000 Characterising the landscape of Roman Britain: a review of the study of Roman Britain 1975–2000, in Hooke, D (ed.), 33–45.

Cornwall County Council 1994 *Cornwall Landscape Assessment 1994*. Truro: Cornwall County Council.

Costen, M 1992a *The Origins of Somerset*. Manchester: Manchester University Press.

Costen, M 1992b Huish and Worth: Old English survivals in a later landscape, *Anglo-Saxon Studies in Archaeol & Hist* **5**, 65–83.

Council for British Archaeology 1993 *The Past in Tomorrow's Landscape*. York: CBA.

Countryside Commission 1991 *Assessment and Conservation of Landscape Character: the Warwickshire Landscape Project approach*. Cheltenham: Countryside Commission.

Countryside Commission 1992 *The Chichester Historic Landscape*. Cheltenham: Countryside Commission.

Countryside Commission 1993 *Landscape Assessment Guidance*. Northampton: Countryside Commission.

Countryside Commission 1994a *Views from the Past: Historic Landscape Character in the English Countryside (Consultation Document)*. Cheltenham: Countryside Commission.

Countryside Commission 1994b *Historic Landscape Assessment – A Methodological Case-Study in Cornwall*. Unpub Report: Countryside Commission, South West Regional Office (Bristol).

Countryside Commission 1994c *The New Map of England: A Celebration of the South Western Landscape*. Cheltenham: Countryside Commission.

Countryside Commission 1996 *Views from the Past: Historic Landscape Character in the English Countryside*. Cheltenham: Countryside Commission.

Countryside Commission and English Nature 1996 *The Character of England: landscape, wildlife and natural features*. Cheltenham/Peterborough.

Crawford, O G S 1953 *Archaeology in the Field*. London: Dent.

Creighton, O. 2002 *Castles and Landscapes*. London: Continuum.

Croft, R A and Mynard, D C 1993 *The Changing Landscape of Milton Keynes*. Aylesbury: Buckinghamshire Archaeological Society.

Darby, H C 1967 The South-Western Counties, in Darby, H C and Welldon Finn, R (eds) *The Domesday Geography of South-West England*. Cambridge: Cambridge Univ Press, 348–392.

Darby, H C. 1973 *A New Historical Geography of England*. Cambridge: Cambridge Univ Press.

Darby, H C 1977 *Domesday England*. Cambridge: Cambridge Univ Press.

Dark, K and Dark, P 1997 *The Landscape of Roman Britain*. Stroud: Tempus.

Darlington, J 2002 European Cultural Paths: a model of co-operation between archaeologists for the management and preservation of cultural landscapes, in Fairclough, G and Rippon, S (eds) *Europe's Cultural Landscape*, 97–106.

Darvill, T 1999 The historic environment, historic landscapes, and space-time action models in landscape archaeology, In Ucko, P and Layton, R (eds), 104–18.

Darvill, T, Gerrard, C and Startin, B 1993 Identifying and protecting historic landscapes, *Antiquity* **67**, 563–74.

Dixon, P and Hingly, R 2002 Historic Landuse Assessment in Scotland, in Fairclough, G and Rippon, S (eds), 85–8.

Dodgshon, R A 1980 *The Origins of British Field Systems: an interpretation*. London: Academic Press.

Dodgshon, R A 1993a West Highland and Hebridean Landscapes: have they a history without runrig? *J Hist Geogr* **19**, 383–98.

Dodgshon, R A 1993b West Highland and Hebridean settlement prior to crafting and the Clearances: a study in stability or change, *Proc Soc Antiq Scotland* **123**, 419–38.

Dodgshon, R A 1994 Rethinking Highland Field Systems, in Foster, S and Smout, T C (eds) *The History of Soils and Field Systems*. Aberdeen, 64–74.

Dodgshon, R A and Butlin, R A 1978 *An Historical Geography of England and Wales*. London: Academic Press.

Donkin, R A 1973 Changes in the Early Middle Ages, in Darby, H C (ed.), 75–135.

Dudley Stamp, L. 1962 *The Land of Britain: its use and misuse*. London: Longman.

Dunning, R W 1974 *Victoria County History of Somerset IV: Kingsbury (East), Pitney, Somerton and Tintinhull Hundreds*. London: Institute of Historical Research.

Dunning, R W 1981 *Victoria County History of Somerset IV: Crewkerne, Martock and South Petherton Hundreds*. London: Institute of Historical Research.

Dunning, R W 1985 *Victoria County History of Somerset V: Whitley (part) and Williton and Freemanors Hundreds*. London: Institute of Historical Research.

Dunning, R W 1992 *Victoria County History of Somerset VI: Andresfield, Cannington and North Petherton Hundreds*. London: Institute of Historical Research.

Dunning, R W 1999 *Victoria County History of Somerset VII: Bruton, Horethorne and North Ferris Hundreds*. London: Institute of Historical Research.

Dyer, C 1985 Power and Conflict in the Medieval Village, in Hooke, D. (ed.) *Medieval Villages*, Oxford, 27–32.

Dyer, C 1990 Dispersed Settlements in Medieval England. A case study of Pendock, Worcestershire, *Med Archaeol* XXXIV, 97–121.

Dyson-Bruce, L, Dixon, P, Hingley, R and Stevenson, J 1999 *Historic Landuse Assessment (HLA): Development and Potential of a technique for Assessing Historic Landuse Patterns. Report of the Pilot Project 1996–1998*. Edinburgh: Historic Scotland/Royal Commission on the Ancient and Historical Monuments of Scotland.

Ecclestone, M 1996 *Dairy Production on the Glastonbury Abbey Demesne 1256–1334.* Unpub MA Dissertation, University of Bristol.

Ede, J with Darlington, J 2002 Lancashire Historic Landscape Characterisation Programme: a report on the context, method and results for the Lancashire, Blackburn with Darwen and Blackpool areas. Preston: Lancashire County Council with English Heritage.

Ellison, A 1983 *Medieval Villages in South-East Somerset.* Bristol: Weston Archaeological Trust.

Emery, F 1967 The Farming Regions of Wales, in Thirsk, J. (ed.) 1967, 113–60.

Emery, F 1973 England *circa* 1600, in Darby, H C (ed.), 248–301.

English Heritage 1997 *Sustaining the Historic Environment: New Perspectives on the Future.* London: English Heritage.

English Heritage, Countryside Commission and English Nature 1993 *Conservation Issues in Strategic Plans.* London: English Heritage, Countryside Commission and English Nature.

English Heritage, Countryside Commission, and English Nature 1996 *Conservation Issues in Local Plans.* London: English Heritage, Countryside Commission and English Nature.

Evans, J 1990 An Archaeological Survey of Skomer, Dyfed, *Proc Prehist Soc* 56, 247–67.

Everitt, A 1979 Country, County and Town: patterns of regional evolution in England. *Trans. Royal Hist Soc,* 5th Ser., 29, 79–108; reprinted in Everitt, A (ed.) 1985, 11–40.

Everitt, A 1985 *Landscape and Community in England.* London: The Hambledon Press.

Everitt, A 1986 *Continuity and Colonisation: the Evolution of Kentish Settlement.* Leicester: Leicester University Press.

Everson, P 1996a Bodiam Castle, East Sussex: a Fourteenth-Century Designed Landscape. In Morgan Evans, D, Salway, P and Thackray, D (eds*), 'The Remains of Distant Times', Archaeology and the National Trust.* London: Occasional Papers of the Society of Antiquaries of London, 66–72.

Everson, P 1996b Bodiam Castle, East Sussex: castle and designed landscape. *Château Gaillard* **16**, 70–84.

Everson, P 1998 'Delightfully surrounded with woods and ponds': field evidence for medieval gardens in England. In Pattison, P (ed.), *There by Design.* Oxford: BAR Brit Ser **267**, 32–38.

Everson, P, Brown, G and Stocker, D 2000 The castle earthworks and landscape context. In Ellis, P (ed.), *Ludgershall Castle, Wiltshire: a Report on the Excavations by Peter Addyman, 1964–1972.* Devizes: Wiltshire Archaeol and Nat Hist Soc Monogr **2**, 97–119.

Fairclough, G 2002 *Historic Landscape Characterisation: Template Project Design for EH-supported county-wide HLC projects.* London: English Heritage.

Fairclough, G and Rippon, S 2002 *Europe's Cultural Landscape: archaeologists and the management of change.* Brussels: Europae Archaelogiae Consilium.

Fairclough, G 1994 Landscapes from the past – only human nature. English Heritage's approach to historic landscapes. *Landscape Issues* **11(i)**, 64–72.

Fairclough, G 1995 The sum of all its parts: an overview of the politics of integrated management in England, in Berry, A Q and Brown, I W (eds) *Managing Ancient Monuments: An Integrated Approach*. Mold: Clwyd County Council, 17–28

Fairclough, G 1999a *Historic Landscape Characterisation: papers presented at an English Heritage seminar, 11th December 1998*. London: English Heritage.

Fairclough, G 1999b Historic Landscape Characterisation: theory, objectives and connections, in Fairclough, G (ed.) 1999a, 3–14.

Fairclough, G 1999c Protecting Time and Space: understanding historic landscape for conservation in England, in Ucko, P and Layton, R (eds), 119–34.

Fairclough, G 2002 *Historic Landscape Characterisation: Template Project Design for EH-supported county-wide HLC projects*. London: English Heritage.

Fairclough, G, Lambrick, G and McNab, A 1999 *Yesterdays World, Tomorrows Landscape (The English Heritage Historic Landscape Project 1992–94)*. London: English Heritage.

Fairclough, G, Lambrick, G and Hopkins, D 2002 Historic Landscape Characterisation in England and a Hampshire case study, in Fairclough, G and Rippon, S (ed.), 69–83.

Fairclough, G and Rippon, S 2002 *Europe's Cultural Landscape: archaeologists and the management of change*. Brussels: Europae Archaeologiae Consilium.

Field, J 1972 *English Field-Name: a dictionary*. London.

Field, J 1993 *A History of English Field Names*. London: Longman.

Finberg, H P R 1951 *Tavistock Abbey: a study in the social and economic history of Devon*. Cambridge: Cambridge Univ Press.

Finch, J 2002 Regionality and medieval landscapes, in Perring, D (ed.) *Town and Country in England: frameworks for archaeological research*. York: CBA Res Rep **134**, 107–15.

Fleming, A 1988 *The Dartmoor Reaves: investigating prehistoric land divisions*. London: Batsford.

Fleming, A 1999 *Swaledale: Valley of the Wild River. Edinburgh*: Edinburgh University Press.

Fleming, A 2001 Dangerous Islands: Fate, Faith and Cosmology, *Landscapes* **2(i)**, 4–21.

Fleming, A and Ralph, N 1982 Medieval Settlement and landuse on Holne Moor, Dartmoor: the landscape evidence. *Med Archaeol* 26, 101–37.

Fleming, R 1983 Domesday estates of the King and the Godwines: a study in Late Saxon politics, *Speculum* 58(iv), 987–1007.

Fleming, R 1991 *Kings and Lords in Conquest England*. Cambridge: Cambridge University Press.

Foard, G 1978 Systematic fieldwalking and the investigation of Saxon settlement in Northamptonshire, *World Archaeol* **9**.

Foard, G and Rippon, S 1998 Managing the historic landscape: 'the Register of Landscapes of Outstanding Historic Interest in Wales', *Landscape Hist* **20**, 99–103.

Ford, W J 1979 Some Settlement Patterns in the Central Region of the Warwickshire Avon', in Sawyer, P H (ed.) *English Medieval Settlement*. London: Edward Arnold, 143–63.

Fox, C 1932 *The Personality of Britain: Its Influence on Inhabitant and Invader in Prehistoric and Early Historic Times*. Cardiff: National Museum of Wales.

Fox, H 1989 Peasant farmers, patterns of settlement and pays: transformations in the landscapes of Devon and Cornwall during the later Middle Ages, in Higham, R (ed) *Landscape and Townscape in the South West*, Exeter, 41–75.

Fox, H 1991 Farming practice and techniques: Devon and Cornwall, in Miller, E (ed.) *The Agrarian History of England and Wales Volume III: 1350–1500*. Cambridge: Cambridge Univ Press, 303–23.

Fox, H 2001 *The Evolution of the Fishing Village: landscape and society along the south Devon coast*. Oxford: Leopard's Head Press.

Fyfe, R M, Brown, A G and Rippon, S 2003 Mid- to Late-Holocene vegetation history of Greater Exmoor, UK: estimating the spatial extent of human-induced vegetation change. *Vegetation History and Archaeobotany* **12**, 215–32.

Fyfe, R M, Brown, A G and Rippon, S in press Continuity and change: environmental evidence from the late prehistoric, Romano-British and medieval period in lowland South West Britain. *Journal of Archaeological Science*.

Gelling, M and Cole, A 2000 *The Landscape of Place-Names*. Stamford: Shaun Tyas.

Gerrard, C and Aston, M forthcoming *The Shapwick Project, 1989–99. Survey, excavation and results*.

Gerrard, S 1997 *Dartmoor: Landscapes through time*. London: Batsford.

Gillard, M 2002 *The Medieval Landscape of the Exmoor Region: enclosure and settlement in an upland fringe*. Unpub PhD thesis, Univ of Exeter.

Glover, J E B, Mawer, A and Stenton, F M 1931 *The Place-Names of Devon Part 1*. English Place-Names Society VIII. Cambridge: Cambridge Univ Press.

Gonner, E C K 1912 *Common Land and Enclosure*. London: Macmillan.

Gray, H L 1915 *English Field Systems*. London: Harvard University Press.

Gwyn, D 2001 the industrial ton in Gwynedd, *Landscape Hist* **23**, 71–89.

Hall, D 1981 The origins of open-field agriculture: the archaeological fieldwork evidence, in Rowley, T. (ed.) *The Origins of Open Field Agriculture*. London: Croom Helm, 22–38.

Hall, D 1992 *The Fenland Project, Number 6: The South-Western Cambridgshire Fens*. East Anglian Archaeol **56**.

Harris, A 1959 *The Open Fields of East Yorkshire*. East Yorkshire Local Hist Ser IX.

Harris, K 1991 *Glastonbury Abbey Records at Longleat House: a summary list*. Somerset Records Soc 81.

Harrison, G V 1984 The South West: Dorset, Somerset, Devon and Cornwall, in Thirsk, J (ed.) *The Agrarian History of England and Wales Volume V.I: 1640–1750*. Cambridge: Cambridge Univ Press, 358–93.

Harrison, J. 1997 *The composite manor of Brent: a study of a large wetland-edge estate up to 1350*. Unpub PhD thesis, Univ of Leicester.

Harvey, P D A 1989 Initiative and authority in settlement change, in Aston, M, Austin, D and Dyer, C (eds.) *The Rural Settlements of Medieval England*, Oxford, 31–43.

Hatcher, J 1970 *Rural Economy and Society in the Duchy of Cornwall 1300–1500*. Cambridge: Cambridge Univ Press.

Hatcher, J 1988 Farming techniques: south-western England, in Hallam, H E (ed.) *The Agrarian History of England and Wales Volume II: 1042–1350*. Cambridge: Cambridge Univ Press, 383–98.

Henderson, C J 1999 The city of Exeter from AD50 to the early nineteenth century, Kain, R & Ravenhill, W (eds) *Historical Atlas of South-West England*. Exeter: Exeter Univ Press, 482–98.

Herring, P 1993 Examining a Romano-British Boundary at Foage, Zennor, *Cornish Archaeol* **32**, 17–28.

Herring, P 1998 *Cornwall's Historic Landscape: presenting a method of historic landscape character assessment*. Truro: Cornwall Archaeol Unit.

Herring, P 1999 Cornwall: How the Historic Landscape Characterisation methodology was developed, in Fairclough, G (ed.) 1999a, 15–32.

Herring, P and Tapper, B P 2002 *The Lynher valley, Cornwall: historical and archaeological appraisal*. Truro: Cornwall Archaeol Unit.

Higham, N 1992 *Rome, Britain and the Anglo-Saxons*. London: Seaby.

Hill, D 1982 The Anglo-Saxons 700–1066 AD, in Aston, M and Burrow, I (eds) *The Archaeology of Somerset*. Taunton: Somerset County Council, 109–18.

Hindle, B 1982 *Medieval Roads*. Aylesbury: Shire

Hinton, D 1997 The 'Scole-Dickleborough Field System' Examined, *Landscape History* **19**, 5–13.

Holt, R. 1987 Whose were the profits of milling corn? The abbots of Glastonbury and their tenants 1086–1350. *Past and Present* **116**, 3–25.

Hook, D 1988 The Warwickshire Arden: the evolution and future of an historic landscape. *Landscape Hist* 10, 51–9.

Hooke, D 1993 *Warwickshire's Historical landscape – The Arden*. Birmingham: private publication.

Hooke, D 1998 *The Landscape of Anglo-Saxon England*. London: Leicester Univ Press.

Hooke, D 2000 *Landscape: the richest historical record*. Society for Landscape Studies.

Horne, P and MacLeod, D 2001 Unravelling a Wharfdale Landscape: A Case Study in Field Enhanced Aerial Survey, *Landscapes* **2(ii)**, 65–82.

Hoskins, W G 1955 *The Making of the English Landscape*. London : Hodder & Stoughton

Hunn, J 1994 *Reconstruction and Measurement of Landscape change: a study of six parishes in the St Albans area*. BAR Brit Ser 236.

Hunn, J 1997 *Lordship and the Landscape: a documentary and archaeological study of the Honor of Dudley c.1066–1322*. Oxford: BAR Brit Ser 264.

Jewell, A 1981 Some Cultivation Techniques in the South-West of England, in Minchinton, W (ed.) *Agricultural Improvement: medieval and Modern*. Exeter: Univ of Exeter Press, 95–111.

Johnson, M 1996 *An Archaeology of Capitalism*. Oxford: Blackwell.

Johnson, N 1999 Context, meaning and consequences: using the map in Cornwall, in Fairclough, G (ed.) 1999a, 117–22.

Johnson, N and Rose, P 1994 *Bodmin Moor: An Archaeological Survey, Volume 1*. London: English Heritage Archaeol Rep **24**.

Jones, B and Mattingly, D. 1990 *An Atlas of Roman Britain*. Oxford: Blackwell.

Jones, R and Page, M 2001 Medieval Settlement and Landscapes in the Whittlewood Area: interim report 2001–2, *Medieval Settlement Research Group Annual Report* 16, 15–25.

Kain, R 1986 *An Atlas and Index of the Tithe Files of Mid-Nineteenth Century England and Wales*. Cambridge: Cambridge Univ Press.

Kain, R J P and Prince, H C 1985 *The Tithe Surveys of England and Wales*. Cambridge: Cambridge Univ Press.

Kain, R J P and Oliver, R R 1995 *The Tithe Maps of England and Wales*. Cambridge: Cambridge Univ Press.

Kain, R J P, Chapman, J and Oliver, R R forthcoming *The Enclosure Maps of England and Wales*. Cambridge: Cambridge Univ Press.

Kain, R and Ravenhill, W (eds) 1999 *Historical Atlas of South-West England*. Exeter: Exeter Univ Press.

Keil, I J E 1964 *The Estates of Glastonbury Abbey in the Later Middle Ages*. Unpub PhD thesis, Univ of Bristol.

Lambrick, G 1992 The importance of the cultural heritage in a green world: towards the development of landscape integrity assessment, in Macinnes, L and Wickham-Jones, C R (eds), 105–27.

Lambrick, G 1999 Hampshire: Historic landscape Characterisation and the Community, in Fairclough, G (ed.) 1999a, 51–66.

Landsberg, S 1996 *The Medieval Garden*. London: British Museum Press.

Leech, R 1975 *Small Medieval Towns in Avon: Archaeology and Planning*. Bristol: Comm for Rescue Archaeol in Avon, Gloucestershire and Somerset.

Leech, R 1981 *Historic Towns in Gloucestershire: Archaeology and Planning*. Bristol: Comm for Rescue Archaeol in Avon, Gloucestershire and Somerset.

Leighley, J (ed.) 1963 *Land and Life: a selection from the writings of Carl Ortwin Sauer*. Berkeley: Univ of California Press.

Lennard, R 1955/6 The demesne of Glastonbury Abbey in the eleventh and twelfth centuries, *Econ Hist Rev* 8, 255–303.

Lennard, R 1975 The Glastonbury estates: a rejoinder, *Econ Hist Rev* **28**, 517–23.

Lewis, C, Mitchell-Fox, P and Dyer, C 1997 *Village, Hamlet and Field: Changing Medieval Settlements in Central England*. Manchester: Manchester Univ Press.

Liddiard, R. 2000 *Landscapes and Lordship: Norman castles in the countryside in medieval Norfolk, 1066–1200*. Oxford: BAR Brit Ser **309**.

Lilley, K. 2002 *Urban Life in the Middle Ages 1000–1450*. Basingstoke: Palgrave.

Longley, D. 2001 Medieval settlement and landscape on Anglesey, *Landscape Hist* **23**, 39–59.

Lucas, G. 1998 A Medieval Fishery on Whittlesea Mere, Cambridgeshire, *Med Archaeol* **XLII** (1998), 19–44.

Macinnes, L 2002a Scotland, in Fairclough, G and Rippon, S (eds), 171–4.

Macinnes, L 2002b The Historic landscape in Scotland: towards a strategy for the future, in T C Smout (ed.) *Understanding the Historical Landscape in its Environmental Setting*. Dalkeith: Scottish Cultural Press, 20–35.

Macinnes, L and Wickham-Jones, C (eds) *All Natural Things: archaeology and the green debate*. Oxford: Oxbow.

Macinnes, L and Wickham-Jones, C 1992b Time-depth in the countryside: archaeology and the environment, in Macinnes, L and Wickham-Jones, C (eds), 1–13.

Mackinder, H.J. 1907 *Britain and the British Seas*. Oxford: Clarendon Press.

Mackney, D, Hodgson, J M, Hollis, J M and Staines, S J 1983: *Legend for the 1:250,000 Soil map of England and Wales: A brief explanation of the constituent soil associations*. Harpenden: Soil Survey of England & Wales.

Maitland, F W 1911 The survival of archaic communities, in Fisher, H A L (ed.) *The collected papers of Frederick William Maitland*. London, 313–65.

Maitland, F W 1921 *Domesday Book and Beyond*. Cambridge: Cambridge Univ Press.

Marshall, W 1808 *The Review and Abstract of the County Reports to the Board of Agriculture from the Several Agricultural Departments of England Volume 1: The Northern Department*. York: Wilson and Sons . Reprinted in 1968, New York: August M Kelly Publishers.

Marshall, W 1818a *The Review and Abstract of the County Reports to the Board of Agriculture from the Several Agricultural Departments of England Volume 2: The Western Department*. York: Wilson & Sons (reprinted in 1968, New York: August M Kelly Publishers.

Marshall, W 1818b *The Review and Abstract of the County Reports to the Board of Agriculture from the Several Agricultural Departments of England Volume 3: The Eastern Department*. York: Wilson & Sons. Reprinted in 1968, New York: August M Kelly Publishers.

Marshall, W 1818c *The Review and Abstract of the County Reports to the Board of Agriculture from the Several Agricultural Departments of England Volume 4: The Midland Department*. York: Wilson & Sons. Reprinted in 1968, New York: August M Kelly Publishers.

Marshall, W 1818d *The Review and Abstract of the County Reports to the Board of Agriculture from the Several Agricultural Departments of England Volume 5: The Southern and Peninsular Departments*. York: Wilson & Sons. Reprinted in 1968, New York: August M Kelly Publishers.

McGlade, J 1999 Archaeology and the evolution of cultural landscapes: towards an interdisciplinary research agenda, in Ucko, P J and Layton, R (eds), 458–82.

McOmish, D, Field, D and Brown, G 2002 *The Field Archaeology of the Salisbury Plain Training Area*. London: English Heritage.

Meddens, F M and Beasley, M 2001 Roman seasonal wetland pasture exploitation near Nash, on the Gwent Levels, Wales, *Britannia* **XXXII**, 141–84.

Miller, K 1999 Using Historic Landscape Characterisation for land management in the Isle of Axholme project, in Fairclough, G (ed.) 1999a, 91–112.

Millett, M 1990 *The Romanization of Britain*. Cambridge: Cambridge Univ Press.

Morrison, A 1900: *Cunning Murrell*. Reprinted 1977, Ipswich: Boydell Press.

Muir, R 1999 *Approaches to Landscape*. London: Macmillan.

Muir, R 2001 *Landscape Detective: discovering a countryside*. Macclesfield: Windgather Press.

Murphy, K 2001 A Prehistoric Field System and Related Monuments on St David's Head and Carn Llidi, Pembrokeshire, *Proc Prehist Soc* 67, 85–99.

Musgrove, D 1997 The medieval exploitation and reclamation of the inland peat moors in the Somerset Levels. *Archaeol. in the Severn Estuary* 8, 89–97.

Musgrove, D 1999 *The Medieval Exploitation of the Peat Moors of the Somerset Levels*. Unpub PhD thesis, University of Exeter.

Musgrove, D 2001 Modelling landscape development in a wetland environment: the medieval peat moors of the Somerset Levels. In Raftery, B and Hickey, J (eds) *Recent Developments in Wetland Research*. Dublin: Department of Archaeology, Univ College, 227–42.

Nayling, N 1998 *The Magor Pill Medieval Wreck*. York: CBA Res Rep 115.

Nayling, N and Caseldine, A 1998 *Excavations at Caldicot, Gwent: Bronze Age Palaeochannels in the Lower Nedern Valley*. York: CBA Res Rep 115.

Oliver, R 1993: *Ordnance Survey Maps: a concise guide for historians*. London: The Charles Close Society.

Oliver, R 1999 Map Evidence of the growth of Exeter during the nineteenth century, in Kain, R and Ravenhill, W (eds), 504–11.

Oosthuizen, S 2003 The roots of the common fields: linking prehistoric and medieval field systems in West Cambridgeshire, *Landscapes* **4(i)**, 40–64.

Oosthuizen, S and Taylor C 2000 'John O'Gaunt's House', Bassingbourn, Cambridgeshire: a fifteenth century landscape, *Landscape Hist* 22, 61–76.

Ordnance Survey 2001 *Roman Britain: historical map and guide*. Southampton: Ordnance Survey.

Padel, O J 1999 Place-Names, in Kain, R. and Ravenhill, W. (eds), 85–94.

Page, M and Jones, R 2000 The Whittlewood Project Interim Report 2000–1, *Medieval Settlement Research Group Annual Report* 15, 10–18.

Pattison, P 1999 Challacomb Revisited, in Pattison, P, Field, D and Ainsworth, S (eds) *Patterns in the Past*. Oxford: Oxbow, 61–70.

Phelps, W 1836 'Survey by Richard Pollard and Thomas Moyle, general surveyors of the King's lands, 1539',in Phelps, W *The History and Antiquities of Somersetshire*, volume **1**. London.

Phillpotts, C 1999 Landscape into townscape: an historical and archaeological investigation of the Limehouse area, east London, *Landscape Hist* **21**, 58–76.

Phythian-Adams, C 1993 Introduction: an Agenda for English Local History, in Phythian-Adams, C (ed.) *Societies, Cultures and Kinship 1580–1850: Cultural Provinces and English Local History*. Leicester: Leicester Univ Press, 1–23.

Postan, M 1952/3 Glastonbury estates in the twelfth century, *Econ Hist Rev* **5**, 358–66.

Postan, M 1956/7 Glastonbury estates in the twelfth century: a reply, *Econ Hist Rev* **9**, 106–18.

Postan, M 1975 Glastonbury estates in the twelfth century: a restatement, *Econ Hist Rev* **28**, 524–7.

Rackham, O 1986 *The History of the Countryside*. London: J M Dent and Sons.

Reaney, P H 1935 *The Place-Names of Essex*. Cambridge: English Place-Names Society Volume **XII**.

Richardson, R E 2002 Using Field-Names, Landscapes **3(ii)**, 70–83.

Riley, H and Wilson-North, R 2001: *The Field Archaeology of Exmoor*. London: English Heritage.

Rippon, S 1991 Early Planned Landscapes in South-East Essex, *Essex Archaeol Hist* **22**, 46–60.

Rippon, S 1993 *Landscape Evolution and Wetland Reclamation Around the Severn Estuary*. Unpub PhD thesis, Univ of Reading.

Rippon, S 1995 Human-Environment Relations in the Gwent Levels: Ecology and the Historic Landscape in a Coastal Wetland, in Cox, M., Straker, V. and Taylor, D. (eds) *Wetlands: Archaeology and Nature Conservation*. London: HMSO, 62–75.

Rippon, S 1996a *The Gwent Levels: the evolution of a wetland landscape*. York: CBA Res Rep **105**.

Rippon, S 1996b *The Gwent Levels Historic Landscape Study: characterisation and assessment of the landscape*. Reading: University of Reading for Cadw: Welsh Historic Monuments & Countryside Council for Wales.

Rippon, S 1997a *The Severn Estuary: landscape evolution and wetland reclamation*. London: Leicester Univ Press.

Rippon, S 1997b Wetland Reclamation on the Gwent Levels: Dissecting a Historic Landscape. In Edwards, N. (ed.) *Landscape and Settlement in Medieval Wales*. Oxford: Oxbow, 13–30.

Rippon, S 1998 Medieval settlement on the North Somerset Levels: the third season of survey and excavations at Puxton, 1998. *Archaeol. in the Severn Estuary* **9**, 69–78.

Rippon, S 1999a The Rayleigh Hills in south-east Essex: patterns in exploitation of a woodland landscape, in Green, S (ed.) *The Essex landscape: in search of its history*. Chelmsford: Essex County Council, 20–8.

Rippon, S 1999b Medieval Settlement on the North Somerset Levels: The Fourth Season of Survey and Excavation at Puxton, 1999, *Archaeol. in the Severn Estuary* **10**, 65–73.

Rippon, S 2000a *Transformation and control: the management of coastal wetlands in North West Europe during the Roman and medieval periods*. London: British Academy.

Rippon, S 2000b The Romano-British exploitation of coastal wetlands. Survey and excavation in the North Somerset Levels, 1993–7. *Britannia* **31**, 69–208.

Rippon, S 2000c *Estuarine Archaeology: The Severn and Beyond*. Exeter: Severn Estuary Levels Research Committee.

Rippon, 2000d The Historic Landscapes of the Severn Estuary Levels, in Rippon, S 2000c, 119–135.

Rippon, S 2001 Reclamation and regional economies of medieval marshland in Britain. In Raftery, B (ed.) *Recent Development in Wetland Research*. Dublin: Univ College Press, 139–48.

Rippon, S 2002 Infield and Outfield: The Early Stages of Marshland Colonisation and the Evolution of Medieval Field Systems, in Lane, T and Coles, J (eds) *Through Wet and Dry: Essays in honour of David Hall*. Sleaford: Lincolnshire Archaeology and Heritage Reports Ser **5**, 54–70.

Rippon, S 2004 A Push Into The Margins? The development of a coastal landscape in North West Somerset (UK) during the late 1st millennium AD. In Hines, J, Lane, A and Redknap, M (eds) *Land, Sea, and Home: Proceedings of a Conference on Viking-period Settlement (Cardiff, July 2001)*. London: Soc for Med Archaeol Monogr.

Rippon, S in press Making the most of a bad situation? Glastonbury Abbey, Meare, and the medieval exploitation of wetland resources in the Somerset Levels. *Medieval Archaeology* **XLVIII**.

Rippon, S, Martin, M and Jackson, A 2001 The Use of Soil Analysis in the Interpretation of an Early Historic Landscape at Puxton in Somerset. *Landscape Hist* 23, 27–38.

Rippon, S and Turner, R 1993 The Gwent Levels Historic Landscape Study, *Archaeol in the Severn Estuary 1993*, 113–17.

Roberts, B K 1987 *The Making of the English Village*. London: Longman.

Roberts, B K and Wrathmell, S 2000a *An Atlas of Rural Settlement in England*. London: English Heritage.

Roberts, B K and Wrathmell, S 2000b Peoples of wood and plain: an exploration of national and local regional contrasts, in Hooke, D. (ed.), 85–95.

Roberts, B K and Wrathmell, S 2002 *Region and Place: a study of English rural settlement*. London: English Heritage.

Rowley, T 1981 *The Origins of Open Field Agriculture*. London: Croom Helm.

Seebohm, F. 1883 *The English Village Community*. London: Longman's, Green and Co.

Sheppard, J.A. 1966 *The Draining of the Marshlands of South Holderness and the Vale of York*. East Yorkshire Local Hist Soc.

Silvester, R J 1988 *The Fenland Project, Number 3: Norfolk Survey, Marshland & Nar Valley*. East Anglian Archaeol **45**.

Silvester, R J 1993 'The addition of more-or-less undifferentiated dots to a distribution map'? The fenland Project in Retrospect, in Gardiner, J (ed.) *Flatlands and Wetlands: current themes in East Anglian archaeology*. East Anglian Archaeol **50**, 34–39.

Silvester, R J 2000 Medieval upland cultivation on Berwyns in North Wales, *Landscape History* **22**, 47–60.

Smout, C 1996 Pre-improvement fields in upland Scotland the case of Loch Tayside, *Landscape Hist* **18**, 47–55.

Stacey, N R 1972 *The Estates of Glastonbury Abbey* c.*1050–1200*. Unpub PhD thesis, Univ of Leeds.

Stamp, L D 1948 *The land of Britain: its use and misuse*. London: Longman, Green and Co.

Stevenson, J B and Dyson Bruce, L 2002 RCAHMS: the Historic Landuse Assessment Project and other Work, in T C Smout (ed.) *Understanding the Historical Landscape in its Environmental Setting*. Dalkeith: Scottish Cultural Press, 51–9.

SVBRG 1996 *The Vernacular Buildings of Shapwick*. Somerset Vernacular Building Research Group.

Swanwick, C, Cole, L and Diacano, M 1999 *Interim Landscape Character Assessment Guidance*. London: Landuse Consultants/Countryside Agency/Scottish Natural Heritage.

Sydes, B 1999 Building on the map: Avon, in Fairclough, G. (ed.) 1999a, 67–82.

Sylvester, D 1969 *The Rural Landscape of the Welsh Borderland*. London: Macmillan.

Tartaglia-Kershaw, L 1999 Integrating Historic landscape Characterisation with Landscape Assessment in Hampshire, in Fairclough, G (ed.) 1999a, 113–16.

Taylor, C 1975 *Fields in the English Landscape*. London: J M.Dent & Sons.

Taylor, C 1979 *Roads and Tracks of Britain*. London: J M.Dent & Sons.

Taylor, C 1983 *Village and Farmstead*. London: G Philip.

Taylor, C C 1989a Somersham Palace, Cambridgeshire, a medieval landscape for pleasure? In Bowden, M, Mackay, D and Topping, P (eds), *From Cornwall to Caithness: Some Aspects of British Field Archaeology, Papers Presented to Norman V. Quinnell*. Oxford: BAR Brit Ser **209**, 211–224.

Taylor, C C 1989b Whittlesford: the study of a river edge village. In Aston, M *et al* (eds) *The Rural Settlements of Medieval England*, Oxford, 207–30.

Taylor, C 2000 Medieval Ornamental Landscapes, *Landscapes* 1(i), 38–55.

Taylor, C and Fowler, P 1978 Roman fields into medieval furlongs?, in Bowen, H C and Fowler, P J (eds) *Early land Allotment in the British Isles*, BAR Brit Ser **48**, 159–62.

Thirsk, J 1964 The Common Fields, *Past and Present* **29**, 3–29.

Thirsk, J 1966 The Origins of the Common Fields, *Past & Present* 33, 142–7.

Thirsk, J 1967a *The Agrarian History of England and Wales, Volume IV 1500–1640*. Cambridge: Cambridge Univ Press.

Thirsk, J 1967b The Farming Regions of England, in Thirsk, J (ed.) 1967, 1–112.

Thirsk, J 2000 *The English Rural Landscape*. Oxford: Oxford Univ Press.

Thompson, M G 1997 *The Polden Hill Manors of Glastonbury Abbey: land and people circa 1260 to 1351*. PhD thesis, Univ of Leicester.

Tilley, C. 1995 Rocks as resources: landscapes and power, *Cornish Archaeol* **34**, 5–57.

Tilley, C. 1996 The power of rocks: topography and monument construction on Bodmin Moor, *World Archaeol* **28(ii)**, 161–76.

Tipping, R 2002 Climatic Variability and 'Marginal' Settlement in Upland British Landscapes: a re-evaluation. *Landscapes* **3ii**, 10–29.

Toulmin Smith, L. 1908 *The Itinerary of John Leland in or about the years 1535–1543, volume 2*. London: George Bell & Sons.

Tuke, J 1800 *General View of the Agriculture of the North Riding of Yorkshire*. London: G. Nichol.

Turner, M E 1978 *A Domesday of English Enclosure Acts and Awards*. Reading: Univ of Reading.

Turner, S 2003 Making a Christian Landscape: Early Medieval Cornwall, in Carver, M (ed.) *The Cross Goes North: Processes of Conversion in Northern Europe, AD300–1300*. York: York Medieval Press, Univ of York, 171–94.

Ucko, P J and Layton, R (eds) *The Archaeology and Anthroplogy of Landscape*. London: Routledge.

Upex, S 2002 Landscape continuity and fossilization of Roman fields into Saxon and medieval landscapes, *Archaeol J* 159, 77–108.

Unwin, T 1983 Townships and Early Fields in North Nottinghamshire, *J Hist Geogr* **9**.iv, 341–6.

Unwin, T 1988 Towards a model of Anglo-Scandinavian Rural Settlement in England, in Hooke, D (ed.) *Anglo-Saxon Settlements*. Oxford: Blackwell, 77–98.

Vinogradoff, P 1892 *Villainage in England: Essays in English Mediaeval History*. Oxford: Oxford Univ Press.

Vinogradoff, P 1905 *The Growth of the Manor*. London: Macmillan.

Vinogradoff, P 1908 *English Society in the Eleventh Century*. Oxford: Oxford University Press.

Wade-Martins, P. 1980 *Village Sites in the Launditch Hundred*. East Anglian Archaeol **10**.

Wainwright, A. 2002 *The Parracombe Fieldscape: Project Report*. Unpub report.

Warner, P 1996 *The Origins of Suffolk*. Manchester: Manchester Univ Press.

Watkins, A 1993 The Woodland Economy of the Forest of Arden in the Later Middle Ages, *Midland History* **XVIII**, 19–36.

Welldon Finn, R and Wheatley, P 1967 Somerset, in Darby, H C and Welldon Finn, R (eds) *The Domesday Geography of South-West England*. Cambridge: Cambridge Univ Press, 132–222.

Whyte, I D 2000 Patterns of parliamentary enclosure of waste in Cumbria: a case study from north Westmorland, *Landscape Hist* **22**, 76–89.

Williams, A 1980 Land and Power in the Eleventh Century: the estates of Harold Godwinson, in Allen Brown, R. (ed.) *Proc. Battle Conference on Anglo-Norman Studies* **III**, 171–87.

Williams, T 1970: *The Draining of the Somerset Levels*. Cambridge: Cambridge Univ Press.

Williamson, T 1987 Early Co-Axial Field Systems on the East Anglian Boulder Clays, *Proc Prehist Soc* 53, 419–31.

Williamson, T 1998 The 'Scole-Dickleborough Field System' Revisisted, *Landscape History* 20, 19–28.

Williamson, T 2002a *The Transformation of Rural England: farming and the landscape 1700–1870*. Exeter: Exeter University Press.

Williamson, T 2002b *The Origins of Hertfordshire*. Manchester: Manchester Univ Press.

Williamson, T 2003 *Shaping Medieval Landscape: Settlement, Society, Environment*. Macclesfield: Windgather Press.

Wills, J 1999 Cotswold AONB: Characterisation, Classification and GIS, in Fairclough, G (ed.) 1999a, 33–40.

Woodside, R and Crow, J 1999 *Hadrian's Wall: an historic landscape*. London: The National Trust.

Wymer, J J and Brown, N R 1995 *Excavations at North Shoebury: settlement and economy in south-east Essex 1500BC–AD1500*. East Anglian Archaeol **75**.

Yearsley, I 1998 *Hadleigh Past*. Chichester: Phillimore.

Index

by Peter Rea

Page numbers in italics refer to illustrations and tables and/or captions.

Court Evan Gwynne castle (Powys) 72, 73

Crawford, O G S 16

cropmarks 29, 122

cultural provinces 18, 19

Cumbria 14

Darby, H C 15

Dartmoor (Devon) 31–4, 35

deer parks 21, 22, 38–51, *58–9*

Devon 15–16, 18, 26, 27, 31–4, 35

Dolgellau Vale 65

Domesday Book 13, 15, 83, 84, 124, 128, 129, 131

Doyle, Sir Arthur Conan 74

droveways and roadside waste *xi*, 14, 21, *29*, 32–4, 39, *40*, *41*, 66, 79, 87–93, 132–42

Dudley Honor of 78

East Anglia 8, 13, 37

enclosure:
  ancient/medieval 38–51, *57*, *58–9*, *62–4*, *83*, 103, *105*, 106, 109, 132–42
  by agreement *83*, 106
  Parliamentary *12*, 13–14, 38–51, 79–80, *82*, *83*, 121
  planned countryside and 8
  post-medieval *12*, 38–51, *57*, *58–9*, *62–4*, 109–10, 132–42

English Heritage 4, 53–5, *58*, 74, 101, 107, 110, 112, 114 (and see historic landscape characterisation)

English Nature 36

Environment Agency 103

Essex 8, 38–51

Exeter (Devon) 7

Exmoor (Devon/Somerset) 78, 81, *82*, *83*, *84*, 119, 120, 121, 124

Everitt, A 1

farming regions 3, 6–14, 15, 17–18, 123–6

Ferlingmere *see* Meare Pool

field barns 14

field-names 3, 28, 52, 77, 81, 83, *84–5*, 134, 137–9

fieldwalking 16, *28–9*, 30, 95, *96*, 98

fishponds 21, *42*, 44

footpaths 9, 73, 107

Ford, Abbot of Glastonbury 137

Fox, C 14, 17

Freake, William 134

Geographical Information Systems (GIS) 25–6, 54, 55, 69, 78, 106–10, 144

Gilpin, Reverend William 65

Glasbury see Bryn-yr-hydd and Glasbury

Glastonbury Abbey (Somerset) 121, 125, 130–1, 132, 142

Godney Moor (Somerset) 134, 142

Godwin/Godwinson family *129*, 130

Goldcliff (Gwent) 93

Gordano, Vale of (Somerset) 119, 120, 121, 122–3

grading historic landscape character 74–6

Gratton (field name) 83, *84*

Gray, H L 14, 15

Grimeston (Orkney) 56, *60*, *61*

Gwent Levels Historic Landscape Study 65–6, *67*, 95, 101

Hadleigh (Essex) *23*, 38–51

Halkyn Mountain (Clwyd) 65

Hampshire 54, *58–9*, 78, 113

Harold II, King 130

Harris, Howell 71

Hay-on-Wye (Powys) 71

Heale (Parracombe, Devon) 83, *84*, *85*, 122

hedges 9, 33, *34*, 73, 110

Herefordshire Unitary Development Plan 113

Heritage Conservation in Lancashire 112

Historic Environment Countryside Advisors 113

historic landscape: definition 3, 19–25

historic landscape characterisation
  Cadw projects 65–74
  English Heritage projects 4, 24, 53–5, 101–15
  uses of 53–69, 74–6, 100–1, 103, 112–14, 115, 144